BIRD HOUSE
MAKE AND MAKEOVER

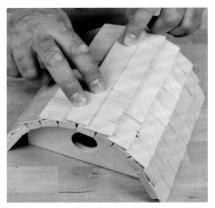

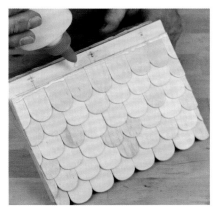

BIRD HOUSE
MAKE AND MAKEOVER
Mix and match to make a unique project

ALAN GOODSELL

Contents

Introduction

This book on bird houses makes it possible for you to build a bird house in the same way as you might buy a new construction house for yourself – by selecting the features you want. The base box is the only feature that all the bird houses have in common and even this can be modified to suit a variety of birds. All the materials for the bird houses can be sourced from DIY stores, craft stores or online. The skill level required is simple and anyone who can craft can build these bird houses.

By combining alternative roof shapes, roof coverings and wall coverings you will have the choice of over 100 different bird houses to make. There are also many different variations of doors, windows and base decorations to choose from. With all these combinations, as well as the paint colour options you could choose, you can build a bird house that is truly unique.

Having a bird house in the garden is extremely satisfying. Firstly, you have the pleasure of building a bespoke home for your bird friends – knowing that you have provided a safe environment for them to rear their young. Then, you have the pleasure of watching the daily comings and goings of the birds after they have conducted their home inspection to make sure your bird house meets their needs. Once moved in, you can watch their daily activities from gathering bedding material through to when the young hatch and the parents start to bring them food. You are most likely to see the flurry of activity at the bird house entrance with wide open mouths waiting for their home delivery meal.

The day will come when the fledglings are old enough to fly the nest. Knowing that you helped them to grow will make this a day you will cherish, especially if you get to see them launch themselves into the air for the first time. Sadly, this day will also mean your bird house will be vacated unless there is another brood to occupy the nest. The end of the breeding season is the time you can get the bird house down, open it up, clean it out and get it ready for the next occupants who will hopefully find it and live in it for the next breeding season.

Enjoy making a custom home for your birds and watching them grow.

Alan

Bird house specifics

THE FIRST THING TO DECIDE BEFORE BUILDING A BESPOKE BIRD HOME IS TO DETERMINE WHAT KIND OF BIRDS YOU WANT TO ATTRACT. THE BIRD HOUSES IN THIS BOOK WILL RESTRICT THE TYPES OF BIRD TO QUITE SMALL ONES, BUT THE SIZE OF THE ENTRY HOLE IS STILL IMPORTANT IN ORDER TO KEEP OUT LARGER BIRDS. IN THIS FIRST CHAPTER YOU CAN FIND OUT ABOUT HOLE SIZE, BIRD SAFETY, BIRD HOUSE LOCATION, TIPS AND PHOTOGRAPHY.

The dimensions

The position and the size of the entrance varies according to the birds you want to host. The size of the hole is critical, even if each one appears quite similar in diameter. Birds may try to squeeze into a hole that is too small and damage their feathers; but if the hole is too large it may let in larger birds who will evict the current residents – and harm or eat their offspring.

Another important dimension is the distance from the hole to the floor. Although the bird houses are all the same size, this distance can easily be altered.

As the floor is inserted inside the walls it can be set at a height that is preferable for your species of bird, but will also maintain the proportions of the house from the outside. See some of the hole-to-floor distances in the chart on pages 12–15.

Hole size
The chart also shows some of the common breeds and hole sizes you will need for their bird home. If you are trying to attract other birds not listed, please research the specifications for hole sizes and ground-to-hole dimensions for that species.

AMERICAN BIRDS	Hole diameter	Hole above floor	Height above ground
Titmice (*Baeolophus*)	1¼in (32mm)	6–8in (150–200mm)	5–15ft (1.5–4.5m)
Nuttall's woodpecker (*Dryobates nuttallii*)	1½in (38mm)	8in (200mm)	5–20ft (1.5–6m)
Downy woodpecker (*Dryobates pubescens*)	1¼in (32mm)	6–8in (150–200mm)	5–15ft (1.5–4.5m)
Hairy woodpecker (*Leuconotopicus villosus*)	1½in (38mm)	8in (200mm)	8–20ft (2.4–6m)
Ash-throated flycatcher (*Myiarchus cinerascens*)	1½in (38mm)	6–8in (150–200mm)	5–15ft (1.5–4.5m)
Great crested flycatcher (*Myiarchus crinitus*)	1¾in (45mm)	6–8in (150–200mm)	5–15ft (1.5–4.5m)
Chickadees (*Poecile*)	1⅛in (30mm)	6–8in (150–200mm)	4–15ft (1.2–4.5m)

AMERICAN BIRDS	Hole diameter	Hole above floor	Height above ground
Prothonotary warbler (*Protonotaria citrea*)	1⅛in (30mm)	4–5in (100–125mm)	4–8ft (1.2–2.4m)
Mountain bluebird (*Sialia currucoides*)	1½in (38mm)	6–8in (150–200mm)	4–6ft (1.2–3m)
Western bluebird (*Sialia mexicana*)	1½in (38mm)	6–8in (150–200mm)	5–10ft (1.5–3m)
Red-breasted nuthatch (*Sitta canadensis*)	1¼in (32mm)	6–8in (150–200mm)	5–15ft (1.5–4.5m)
White-breasted nuthatch (*Sitta carolinensis*)	1¼in (32mm)	6–8in (150–200mm)	12–20ft (3.6–6m)
Pygmy nuthatch (*Sitta pygmaea*)	1in (25mm)	6in (150mm)	3–25ft (1–7.5m)
Yellow-bellied sapsucker (*Sphyrapicus varius*)	1½in 38mm)	8in (200mm)	10–20ft (3–6m)

AMERICAN BIRDS	Hole diameter	Hole above floor	Height above ground
Tree swallow (*Tachycineta bicolor*)	1½in (38mm)	4–6in (100–150mm)	5–15ft (1.5–4.5m)
Violet-green swallow (*Tachycineta thalassina*)	1½in (38mm)	2–5in (50–125mm)	10–15ft (3–4.5m)
Bewick's wren (*Thryomanes bewickii*)	1¼in (32mm)	4–6in (100–150mm)	5–10ft (1.5–3m)
Carolina wren (*Thryothorus ludovicianus*)	1½in (38mm)	4–6in (100–150mm)	5–10ft (1.5–3m)
House wren (*Troglodytes aedon*)	1in (25mm)	2–6in (50–150mm)	5–10ft (1.5–3m)

EUROPEAN BIRDS	Hole diameter	Hole above floor	Height above ground
Blue tit (*Cyanistes caeruleus*)	1in (25mm)	2–6in (50–150mm)	3–15ft (1–5m)
Pied flycatcher (*Ficedula hypoleuca*)	1⅛in (30mm)	6–8in (150–200mm)	Above 8ft (2.5m)
Great tit (*Parus major*)	1⅛in (30mm)	6–8in (150–200mm)	3–15ft (1–5m)
House sparrow (*Passer domesticus*)	1¼in (32mm)	1½in (38mm)	Above 6.5ft (2m)
Tree sparrow (*Passer montanus*)	1⅛in (30mm)	6–8in (150–200mm)	Above 6.5ft (2m)
Nuthatch (*Sitta europaea*)	1¼in (32mm)	1½in (38mm)	Above 9.5ft (3m)
Starling (*Sturnus vulgaris*)	1¾in (45mm)	6–8in (150–200mm)	Above 8ft (2.5m)

Safety

It is quite a common practice to combine nest boxes and feeders in one bird house, but this can attract predators, so it is probably best to keep nest boxes and feeders separate. After all, who wants to live above a restaurant or next to a noisy bar?

Perches are often seen on bird houses and while it is nice to see your new tenants sitting outside their front door, this can also attract unwanted guests. You don't want to give predators a good vantage point to look in the home and see if there are any tasty little morsels in there. Without a perch the birds will be able to get in and out with no problem and rodents and other predators will go and look elsewhere for their snacks.

A bird house can be mounted on a building, fence or tree and should be placed at the height recommended in the chart (see pages 12–15). The best method is to mount the bird house on a standalone pole, which predators would need to climb to gain access to the bird house. They can be prevented access by greasing the pole so they only climb so far, then slide down again. Placing an inverted cone-shaped predator baffle on the pole creates a virtually impossible barrier that will further discourage predators.

Another unwanted set of guests could be bees or wasps – and a way to discourage them is to wax the inside of the roof of the bird house so their nests will not stick to it. They will soon find another home.

Location

The location you choose for your bird house is important and you should also make sure it is placed in a way that the birds will like. Make sure that birds are protected from predators (see Safety box, left) and that the bird house is the correct height above the ground for the species of bird you want to attract.

You should also ensure that they have an easy flight path to the entrance hole so they can shelter quickly from adverse weather. Make every effort to place the entrance hole away from the prevailing wind; birds don't like a howling gale in their home. If you are in a warm climate, position the front of the house north so that the nest inside is kept cool in the shadiest place possible.

Some birds like their home to be under the cover of trees and others in an open space. If the house is hung from a tree make sure it is far away from the trunk; many predators are climbers too.

If you mount your bird house on a tree, be careful of predators

A fence can be a convenient place to mount your bird house

The bird house mounted on a single pole is the safest place for it

If you hang your bird house from a tree branch, make sure it is away from the trunk

Tips

Can I take a look inside the bird house?
Yes, but be careful not to do it too often as this may scare the birds away. If the birds are in there, they will be sitting tight on their nest; if they are away, it is a good time to count the eggs, if there are any. Do not be tempted to put your fingers inside the house as this will certainly make the birds leave. To watch your bird house, consider using the miniature Wi-Fi camera option described below.

Can I clean the bird house?
No, not while the birds are in there. Nobody wants a stranger coming into their house, so you should offer your tenants the same privacy and respect, and wait until they have vacated. Remember that some species may want to reside in the house for two broods in a season. At the end of the season you will want to clean out ready for next year. Make sure you wear surgical gloves and a dust mask as birds' nests can house fungus and a variety of parasites such as fleas, lice and ticks. Open the box and empty it into a plastic bag and seal it quickly ready for disposal.

Photographing birds

It is possible to get miniature Wi-Fi remote cameras that you could fit inside the bird house; they are designed for security or spy usage, but are ideal for bird-viewing purposes. These cameras are easy to mount; some are simply fixed by magnets. Although the camera may have its own power supply it will only last a short time, so you will want to thread a power cable from a larger external battery supply to the camera. The camera also needs to have night vision as it will be quite dark in the bird house. The resulting photos will have that grey look, but will be perfectly viewable. If you can, rig up a lamp inside the bird house that you can turn on and off remotely, and then you can benefit from full colour videos and photos. All this live action inside the birds' home can be viewed and stored remotely on your mobile device.

Another type of photography you could try is to shoot from outside the bird house so you can see the parents coming and going. If you are lucky, you might even be able to catch the first flight of the fledglings. Set up a camera indoors on a tripod by a window that has good visibility to the bird house. You can sit by the camera, with a remote control, and wait for activity, then start shooting. The camera will need to be set on a fast shutter speed to freeze the movement of the birds and also allow faster shooting in multiple-shot mode.

You will need a bright day with good light, preferably with a fast zoom lens that will let you get a shot in close to the bird house. You could set a fast ISO speed to get a similar result; the downfall of the high ISO is a grainier photo, but modern cameras have got a lot better and most people wouldn't notice any graininess.

Experiment with shooting to see the kind of results you can expect, then spend some time watching your feathery tenants as they come and go and capturing their movements to show your friends.

This tiny Wi-Fi camera could be installed inside the bird house. The live or still images from it can be viewed and stored on your mobile device

If you are lucky you could get a shot like this

Mount your camera on a tripod and use a remote control to reduce the likelihood of camera shake

Frame your shot carefully and wait for the birds. You might want to sit down as this could take quite some time

If you are patient, you might be able to get a shot like this

The basic box

THE FIRST PART OF THE BIRD HOUSE YOU NEED TO BUILD IS THE BASIC BOX. YOU WILL NEED JUST A FEW WOODWORKING TOOLS AND SKILLS TO COMPLETE THIS. IF YOU KNOW WHAT BIRDS YOU WANT TO ATTRACT, YOU CAN WORK OUT THE HOLE-TO-FLOOR DISTANCE YOU REQUIRE AND ADJUST THIS ACCORDINGLY.

Starting out

Having a basic box means you can mix and match the style of roof you want, and even make different roofs for the same box. The bird house is designed to be a practical home for birds, but can just as easily be made as a decorative item for the home or garden by not making a hole to allow the birds to come in. When the box has been made, you can decide on any particular treatment you want for the walls, doors, windows or other features you may wish to add.

What you need

SIDE WALLS
2 @ plywood ⅜in (10mm) thick x 6in (150mm) wide x 5½in (140mm) high

FRONT AND BACK WALLS
2 @ plywood ⅜in (10mm) thick x 5¼in (132mm) wide x 5⅛in (130mm) high

FLOOR
1 @ plywood ⅜in (10mm) thick x 5¼in (132mm) x 5¼in (132mm)

- Hammer or nail gun and ¾in (19mm) long nails, pins or brads
- 120 grit sandpaper (and wooden block)
- Waterproof glue
- Pencil
- Tape measure
- Combination square
- Saws
- Drill and drill bit
- Nail punch
- Clamp

Dimensions

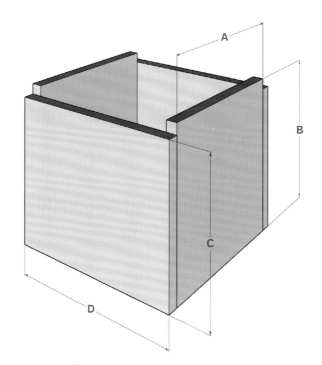

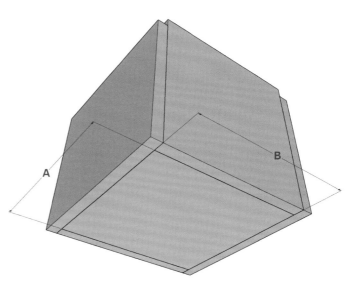

Front and side wall dimensions

A 5¼in (132mm)

B 5½in (140mm)

C 5⅛in (130mm)

D 6in (150mm)

Floor dimensions

A 5¼in (132mm)

B 5¼in (132mm)

Sawing and nailing

The bird house is made from plywood as it is more stable than wood. Try and use marine grade plywood if you can, but you can also get good grade plywood from hobby stores. Although it is a little more expensive than buying from DIY stores it will come in smaller, more manageable pieces that will be easier to cut. Make sure you don't get treated plywood as the chemicals may be a health hazard for the birds. The bird houses will be painted so they will be waterproof.

You can use a small sheet of plywood from the craft store to make the bird box

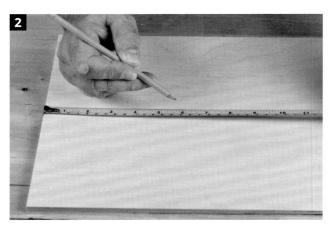

Mark out the sizes of the pieces for the sides and bottom of the bird box

Use a square to extend the marks and make sure they are square to the edge of the plywood

There are a number of ways to cut the plywood. If you are a woodworker you will probably have a tablesaw but if not, then invest in a hand panel saw with hard point teeth and a clamp to hold the wood to your table (bench) while it is being cut. You will also need some sandpaper; 120 grit will work for all the sanding you will be doing. Wrap the sandpaper around a wooden block and use it to round off edges and smooth any discrepancies. Use a sharp pencil and a combination square to mark where you want to cut the wood and carefully cut to the outside of the line to ensure the pieces fit together. There are only five pieces to cut so it shouldn't take too long. When the cutting is done, a quick sanding of the edges will take off any sharp corners.

Cut the plywood on the line either with a hand panel saw…

…or a tablesaw, if you have one

When you have all the pieces cut to size, mark them so you know if they are front, back, sides or bottom

Sand the edges of the plywood to round off edges and avoid getting splinters

The pieces of wood are then held together with waterproof glue and small nails called pins. I used ¾in (19mm) long pins (called brads in the US). If you are going to hammer the pins in manually it is a good idea to drill small holes in the first piece of wood to make it easier to hold them in place when hammering. An alternative to the hammer is to use a small electric nail gun. This is extremely convenient to use and relatively inexpensive. You will be surprised how many other things the nail gun can be used for, especially as many of them can take staples too.

To use the nail gun, the item it is nailing into needs to be held firmly to give resistance to the nailing action. If you don't do this, the pin will not be driven home completely. However, this isn't really a problem as the head of the nail can be tapped flush with a hammer. To finish the job, a pin punch can be used to drive in the nail so it is recessed below the surface of the wood, then filler applied to the recess. The bird houses are not fine woodworking, however, so you can just drive the nail flush. The paint that will be used to decorate the bird house later will cover up the nail (see pages 136–43).

Making the box

Place a side edgeways on the bench and apply a line of glue along its edge. Now place the front on it, making sure the bottom edges line up and the front piece's edge is flush with the side. Drive the nails home, then repeat the process on the other side. Turn the assembled piece over then glue and nail on the back of the box.

Mark the positions where you would like the nails to go. Ensure they are in the middle of the piece of plywood you are going to nail into

If you are going to hammer the nails in, it is useful to drill a small hole first to start them off

Glue the edges of the plywood before nailing

Start hammering the nails in...

...and drive the nails in flush with the surface of the plywood

A faster option than hammering is to use a small nail gun. This is inexpensive and easy to use

Position the head of the nail gun carefully; it may drive the nail in differently to how you might expect

With the bench behind the work to provide support, drive the nails all the way in

If the nails don't drive in all the way, use a nail punch to finish the job

With the walls nailed and glued it is time for the bottom piece

The last thing to do is to apply glue around the edges of the bottom. Place the bottom inside the box and align it with the bottom edges of the walls and nail in the pins. If you wanted to attract birds with a different hole-to-floor distance (see chart on pages 12–15), then you would simply slide the floor further up inside the walls and secure in the position that you require.

The bottom piece can be set at any height you wish, depending on the hole-to-floor dimension of your chosen bird house

In this bird house the floor is set right at the bottom of the walls…

…then glued and nailed in place

The basic bird box is now finished, ready for your choice of roof and wall treatment

Roofs are attached to the base box using screws. In the front and rear corners, mark and drill the holes for the screws. This picture shows a basic box with a brick wall treatment being fitted with a tile roof

Building the roofs

ROOFS COME IN MANY SHAPES AND STYLES, BUT I HAVE SELECTED FOUR TYPES OF ROOF FOR YOU TO CHOOSE FROM FOR YOUR BIRD HOUSE. NOT ONLY ARE THESE ROOFS ATTRACTIVE AND POPULAR ROOF STYLES, BUT THEY ARE ALSO EASY TO MAKE, ESPECIALLY FOR THE INEXPERIENCED WOODWORKER.

Pitch roof

This is the classic house roof. If you ask a child to draw a house this is the roof style they will most likely come up with: angled roofs with gables. The angle of the pitch for houses usually depends on the type of weather conditions it will encounter: steep for places with snow and shallow for places that have more clement weather, or perhaps an architect's whim just for the design of the house. For our bird houses the simplest pitch is 45°, which will create a 90° angle at the peak of the roof for the ridge cap. This means that a simple corner moulding can be used for the ridge cap.

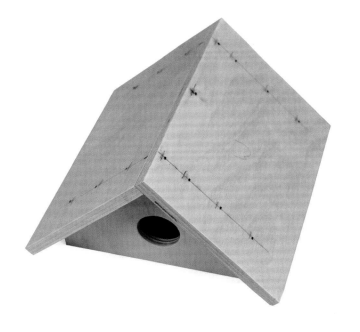

What you need

FRONT AND BACK GABLES
2 @ plywood ⅜in (10mm) thick x 5¼in (132mm) wide x 3½in (90mm) high

ROOF PIECE (NARROW)
1 @ plywood ⅜in (10mm) thick x 5in (125mm) wide x 8in (200mm) long

ROOF PIECE (WIDE)
1 @ plywood ⅜in (10mm) thick x 5⅜in (136mm) wide x 8in (200mm) long

- Hammer and nails or nail gun and ¾in (19mm) long nails, pins or brads
- 120 grit sandpaper (and wooden block)
- Waterproof glue
- Pencil
- Tape measure
- Combination square
- Saws
- Mitre box
- Hole saw of the diameter you require
- Drill
- Vice
- Clamp

Dimensions

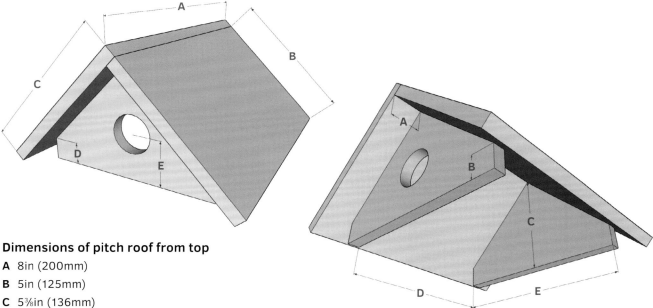

Dimensions of pitch roof from top
A 8in (200mm)
B 5in (125mm)
C 5⅜in (136mm)
D ¾in (19mm)
E 1⅜in (35mm)

Dimensions of pitch roof from underside
A 1in (25mm)
B ¾in (19mm)
C 6in (150mm)
D 5¼in (135mm)
E 3⅞in (96mm)

Making the pitch roof

Cut the pieces of wood to size and then cut the 45° angles on the gables to form the pitch. To do this, mark the angle ¾in (19mm) up from the bottom on each side of the gable end, then draw a 45° line from each mark to where they will meet at the ridge point. Choose your method to saw these angles. When cut on both pieces, put one piece aside and hold the other firmly ready to cut its hole.

Cut the pieces to size and mark them so they get assembled correctly. Mark 'W' and 'N' to denote wide and narrow on the roof pieces. The gable ends are the same size so don't need marking

On the gable ends mark a line ¾in (19mm) up from the bottom on each side

Now mark a 45° line from this mark on both sides to create the 90° pitch

Mark a cross 1⅜in (35mm) up from the bottom and in the centre of the plywood width for the centre of the entrance hole

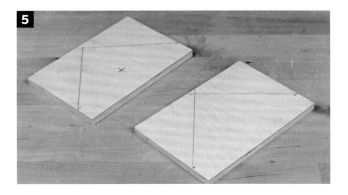

With both pieces of wood marked, you can now cut and drill them

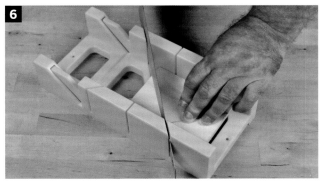

A mitre box can ensure an accurate 45° angle cut

The centre of the hole is 1⅜in (35mm) up from the bottom and you need to cut a 1¼in (32mm) hole with a hole saw. Place the hole saw in a power drill and position the drill bit on the marked centre of the hole. Start the drill and drill until the hole saw has cut about halfway through the wood. Then turn the wood around and position the drill bit in the drilled hole and cut through the wood until the hole saw cuts meet. This technique will reduce the likelihood of tearout (exit-hole splinters). If you do not have a power drill and hole saw, you can cut the hole with an inexpensive coping saw. However, the result is unlikely to be exactly round and is much more time consuming.

Using a hole saw, line up the drill on the marked cross and drill halfway into the plywood

Turn the workpiece around in the vice and insert the drill into the hole drilled from the other side and drill the hole all the way through

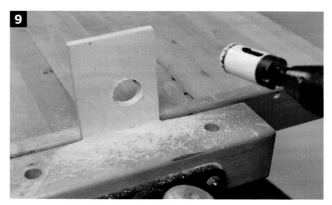

Drilling from both sides prevents the wood from splintering and creates a cleaner hole

Sand off any rough edges around the outside edges of the wood...

...and also in the hole

Draw lines for the positions of the nails in all the pieces and drill nail holes if you are hammering the nails in manually. Then place the gable ends on top of the basic box you built earlier. Having the gable pieces on top of the box will hold them in place while attaching the roof pieces. Now glue along one side of the angled tops of the gable pieces ready to attach the roof piece. Position the shorter of the two roof pieces flush with the top of the other angled top and centred front to back. The previously marked pencil lines will ensure that the nails will be in the correct position.

Now nail the roof piece in place. Repeat the process on the other, longer roof piece side, but this time make sure that the roof piece edge lines up with the roof piece you have just attached. This ensures that the roof is the same length on both sides and there is a 90° angle on the top without the need to cut a mitre. Lastly, drill holes in the lower left and right edges of the front and back so the top can be screwed to the basic box.

The pitch roof is now complete and ready for the roof treatment you desire.

Place the gable ends on the base and mark a line where to nail into the roof pieces

Extend the lines across both roof pieces

Place the gable end on the roof piece and mark the positions of the nails. The spacings are not critical

Use the first piece as a guide to mark the other roof pieces

Glue the edges of the gable end and place the narrow roof piece on top so its edge lines up with the gable end's ridge, then nail it in place

Glue the edges of the gable on the other side and place the roof piece on top. Align its top edge with the top edge of the other roof piece and nail in place

With the wide and narrow roof pieces in place, the roof now measures the same both sides

The underside of the roof shows the design and how the parts fit together

Slant roof

The slant roof is a common roof style for bird houses. It is attractive and relatively simple to make. The slant roof will work with any of the roof type treatments – from tile all the way to solar. Simply adjust the height of the barge boards to suit the style of treatment: deep like a tray for grass and flush for a tile treatment. If using a tray type roof, it may be advisable to drill a couple of holes in the lower side to allow rainwater to drain out.

What you need

SIDE WALLS
2 @ plywood ⅜in (10mm) thick x 6in (150mm) wide x 3⅜in (85mm) high

FRONT
1 @ plywood ⅜in (10mm) thick x 5¼in (132mm) wide x 3⅜in (85mm) high

BACK
1 @ plywood ⅜in (10mm) thick x 5¼in (132mm) wide x 2⅛in (55mm) high

ROOF PIECE
1 @ plywood ⅜in (10mm) thick x 7½in (190mm) wide x 8in (200mm) long

For list of tools required, see page 29

Dimensions

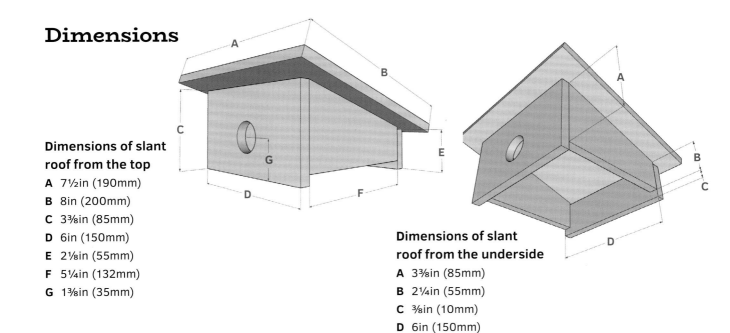

Dimensions of slant roof from the top
- **A** 7½in (190mm)
- **B** 8in (200mm)
- **C** 3⅜in (85mm)
- **D** 6in (150mm)
- **E** 2⅛in (55mm)
- **F** 5¼in (132mm)
- **G** 1⅜in (35mm)

Dimensions of slant roof from the underside
- **A** 3⅜in (85mm)
- **B** 2¼in (55mm)
- **C** ⅜in (10mm)
- **D** 6in (150mm)

Making the slant roof

Cut the pieces of wood to size and then cut the angles on the sides. Mark the angle 3⅜in (85mm) up from the bottom on the front of the sides and 2¼in (55mm) up from the back. Draw a line joining the two marks together. Choose your method to saw the angles and when cut on both pieces, put one piece aside and hold the other firmly ready to cut its hole. Draw lines for the positions of the nails in all the pieces and drill nail holes first if hammering the nails in manually.

Place the four base pieces on top of the basic box you built earlier. Take away the front piece and glue the edge of the side pieces it will attach to. Place the front piece back in position and nail it in place. Repeat the process for the rear piece. Having the pieces on top of the box will hold them square. Now glue along tops of the box ready to attach the roof piece.

Cut all pieces to size and mark them so you know which pieces are which

Mark lines 3⅜in (85mm) up from the bottom on the front of the side pieces and 2¼in (55mm) up from the back

Draw a line joining the two marks together

Mark both sides and cut them ready to make the slant roof

Place the front and a side on top of the box and glue and nail it in place. Repeat with the other side

Glue the back edges of the sides...

...then nail them back in place

Mark the position for the line of nails on the roof

Then mark where the nails will be placed

Continue marking all around the roof for the nail positions

Run a line of glue around the top edges of the roof base

Position the roof piece centred on top of the roof box. The previously marked pencil lines will ensure that the nails will be in the correct position. Now nail the roof piece in place.

I realized now that I hadn't drilled the hole in the front piece. I could take the roof apart and drill it, but I decided to take a chance that the hole saw wouldn't tearout too much and drilled it all the way through the wood from the front with the roof assembled. I marked the centre of the hole 1⅜in (35mm) up from the bottom to cut a 1¼in (32mm) hole with a hole saw. I placed the hole saw in a power drill and positioned the drill bit on the marked centre of the hole. I started the drill and drilled until the hole saw cut all the way through. I was lucky that the tearout was minimal.

The slant roof is now complete and ready for the roof treatment you desire.

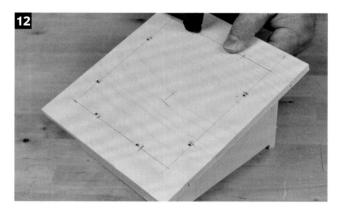

Place the roof piece on top and nail it in place

It is best to drill the hole in the front before assembly. Luckily there was little tearout drilling it all the way through from one side

Sand the rough edges and around the hole

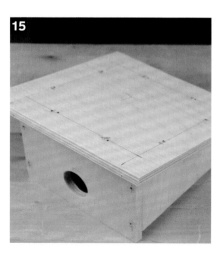

The finished roof is ready for its roof treatment

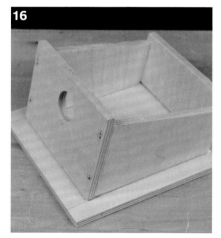

The underside of the roof shows how it is assembled

Curved roof

This roof style is reminiscent of a barn-type roof and is easier to construct than it looks. The curved shape is made up of a series of narrow flat pieces that look like a curve when assembled together. The gaps between the pieces of roof are minimal and when covered with a tile or shingle they will be hidden and watertight. However, it might pay to put a waterproof membrane over the roof to make sure it is actually waterproof – and this can be as simple as a piece of plastic cut from a rubbish bag.

What you need

FRONT AND BACK
2 @ plywood ⅜in (10mm) thick x 5¼in (132mm) wide x 3¼in (85mm) high

NARROW ROOF PIECES
8 @ plywood ⅜in (10mm) thick x ¾in (19mm) x 8in (200mm)

WIDE ROOF PIECES
2 @ plywood ⅜in (10mm) thick x 2¾in (70mm) x 8in (200mm)

For list of tools required, see page 29

Dimensions

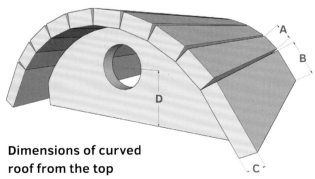

Dimensions of curved roof from the top

A   ¾in (19mm)
B   2¾in (70mm)
C   ⅜in (10mm)
D   1⅜in (35mm)

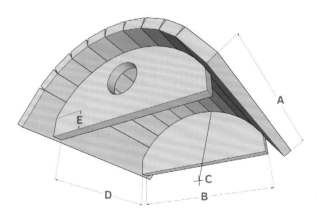

Dimensions of curved roof from the underside

A   8in (200mm)
B   6in (150mm)
C   6½in (165mm) dia.
D   5¼in (132mm)
E   1⅛in (30mm)

Making the curved roof

Cut the pieces of wood to size and then cut the curve on the front and back. This curve was marked using a coffee container lid that is 6½in (165mm) in diameter. Make a mark 1⅛in (30mm) up from the bottom on the front on both sides. Then place the lid on the marks and draw the circular line on the front and back pieces. The ridge should then be around 3in (75mm) up from the bottom.

Choose your method to saw the curve. I used a scrollsaw but if you don't have one, an inexpensive coping saw will make the same cut. Finish by smoothing the curve with sandpaper. When cut on both pieces put one piece aside and hold the other firmly ready to cut its hole. The centre of the hole is 1⅜in (35mm) up from the bottom. I am cutting a 1¼in (32mm) diameter hole with a hole saw. You need to place the hole saw in a power drill and position the drill bit on the marked centre of the hole. Start the drill and drill until the hole saw has cut about halfway through the wood. Then turn the wood around, position the drill bit in the drilled hole and cut through the wood until the hole saw cuts meet.

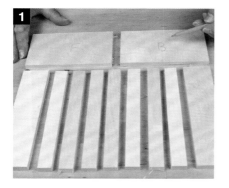

Cut all pieces to size and mark them so you know which pieces are which

Sand the edges of all the pieces to make them smooth

Mark a line 1⅛in (30mm) up from the bottom on the front…

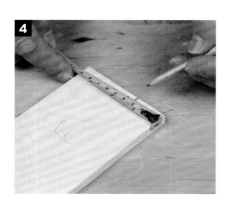

…and do the same the other side

Use a lid of about 6½in (165mm) diameter (or similar), to draw the curve between the two marks

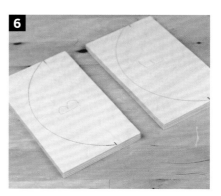

Mark the curve on both roof ends

Mark the centreline for the hole

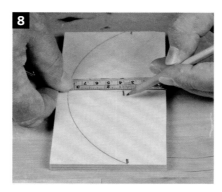

Then mark the hole centre 1⅜in (35mm) up from the bottom to make a cross

Use your chosen sawing method (such as a coping saw), to cut the curve on the roof end

Repeat the cut on the other end piece

Place the plywood end piece in a vice and with a hole saw, drill halfway through

Turn the wood around in the vice and finish cutting the hole from the other side

Sand the hole edges to make sure they are smooth

Draw lines for the positions of the nails in all the pieces. Drill the nail holes first if you are hammering the nails in manually, then place the front and back on top of the basic box to hold them square and in position. Mark the centre point of the roof on the front and back pieces: this will be the starting place to begin attaching the roof. Place a smear of glue on one side of the centreline on the front and back. Position one of the narrow roof pieces equidistant front to back and its edge on the centreline; now nail it in place. Repeat the process for the roof piece on the other side of the centreline. Continue doing this with all eight pieces and the curved roof is formed.

Glue and nail on the wide roof pieces and they will attach to the roof ends and overhang the side walls. Lastly, drill holes in the lower left and right edges of the front and back so the top can be screwed to the basic box.

The roof is now complete and ready for the roof treatment you desire.

Mark a centreline at the top of the roof end then…

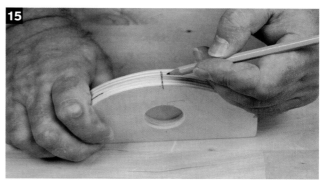

…extend the line across the top of both roof ends

Place the roof ends on top of the basic box, then glue and place one of the narrow roof pieces on top with its edge on the centreline and nail it in place. Make sure it is centred front-to-back

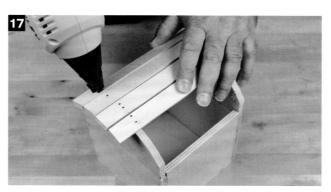

Glue and place the narrow roof pieces next to each other and nail them in place

The last pieces are the wide ones. Glue and nail them in place next to the last narrow pieces. They overhang the roof so there is only enough space for a nail at the top; glue will hold it in place

The underside of the roof shows how it is assembled

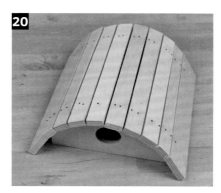

The finished roof is ready for its roof treatment

Flat roof

The flat roof is a common type of roof seen in hot climates. We can take advantage of that to show you a roof treatment that is well suited to a solar panel. This will provide the power for a bird bath fountain that is located near the bird house. The flat will suit other roof treatments and, like the slant roof, it may be advisable to drill drain holes in it for rainwater to escape. Like the slant roof, a simple adjustment in the height of the barge boards will provide for other roof treatments; the tile and shingle treatment is not recommended though.

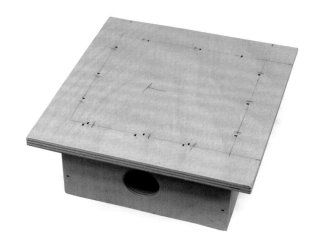

What you need

SIDE WALLS
2 @ plywood ⅜in (10mm) thick x 6in (150mm) wide x 2⅝in (65mm) high

FRONT AND BACK
2 @ plywood ⅜in (10mm) thick x 5¼in (132mm) wide x 3in (75mm) high

ROOF PIECE
1 @ plywood ⅜in (10mm) thick x 7½in (190mm) wide x 7½in (190mm) long

For list of tools required, see page 29

Dimensions

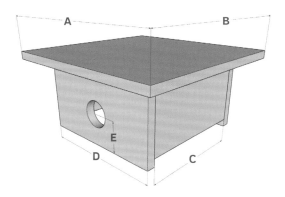

Dimensions of the flat roof from the top

A 7½in (190mm)   **D** 6in (150mm)

B 7½in (190mm)   **E** 1⅜in (35mm)

C 5¼in (132mm)

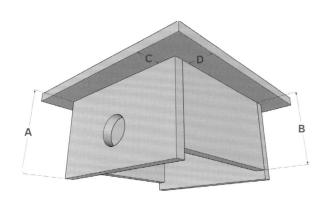

Dimensions of the flat roof from the underside

A 3in (75mm)   **C** ¾in (19mm)

B 2⅝in (65mm)   **D** ¾in (19mm)

Making the flat roof

Cut the pieces of wood to size and proceed to cut the hole in the front. The centre of the hole is 1⅜in (35mm) up from the bottom and I am cutting a 1¼in (32mm) hole with a hole saw. Place the hole saw in a power drill and position the drill bit on the marked centre of the hole. Start the drill and drill until the hole saw has cut about halfway through the wood. Then turn the wood around, position the drill bit in the drilled hole and cut through the wood until the hole saw cuts meet.

Cut all pieces to size and mark them so you know which pieces are which

Mark the centreline for the hole

Then mark the hole centre 1⅜in (35mm) up from the bottom to make a cross

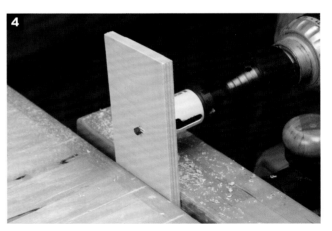

Place the plywood end in a vice and with a hole saw drill halfway through

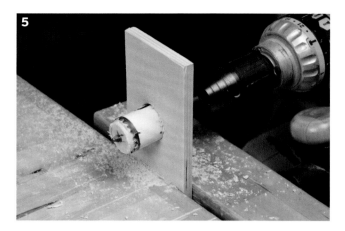

Place the gable ends on the base and mark a line where to nail into the roof pieces

Extend the lines across both roof pieces

If hammering the nails in manually, draw lines for the position of the nails in all the pieces and drill nail holes. Then place the four base pieces on top of the basic box you built earlier. Take away the front piece and glue the edge of the side pieces it will attach to. Place the front back in position and nail it in place. Repeat the process for the rear piece. Having the pieces on top of the box will hold them square. Now, glue along tops of the box ready to attach the roof piece. Position the roof

piece centred on top of the roof box; the previously marked pencil lines will ensure that the nails will be in the correct position. Now nail the roof piece in place. Lastly, drill holes in the lower left and right edges of the front and back so the top can be screwed to the basic box.

The flat roof is now complete and ready for the roof treatment you desire.

Place the roof ends to fit on top of the basic box, then glue and nail a roof side to the ends

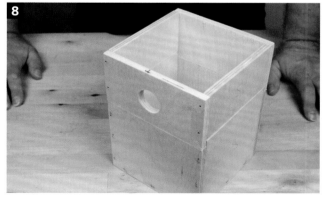

Glue and nail the other side to the roof ends. The roof box can still be removed

9

Place the flat roof piece on the bench and centre the roof box on top. Now draw a line around the roof box so the nail positions can be marked

10

Flip the flat roof piece over and mark the line for the nails

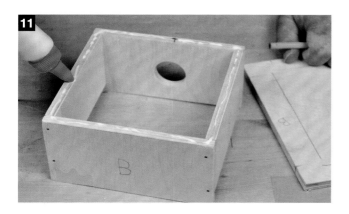

11

Glue the top edge of the roof box

12

Place the flat roof piece on top of the roof box and nail it in place

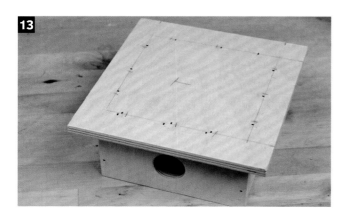

13

The finished roof is ready for its roof treatment

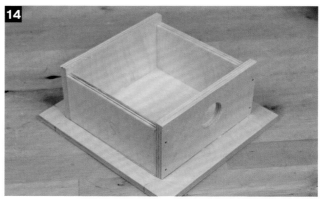

14

The underside shows how the roof is assembled

Roof treatments

ROOFS ON HOUSES ARE DESIGNED TO MAKE THE BUILDING WATERPROOF AND OURS DO EXACTLY THE SAME JOB. DIFFERENT TYPES OF ROOF TREATMENT EVOLVED THROUGH HISTORY, AND WERE USUALLY BASED ON THE MATERIALS THAT WERE AVAILABLE LOCALLY. THESE DAYS MOST MATERIALS ARE AVAILABLE EVERYWHERE SO THE STYLE OF A ROOF IS A MATTER OF PERSONAL CHOICE.

What you need

- Angle cutters
- Saw
- Waterproof wood glue
- Hot glue gun with glue
- Hammer and nails or nail gun and nails (various sizes)
- Pencil
- Sharp knife
- 100 grit sandpaper (and wooden block)
- Tape measure
- Ruler
- Masking tape
- Combination square
- Saws
- Mitre box
- Drill
- Screwdriver
- Clips
- Relevant materials for each roof treatment

About materials and tools

The materials used in the previous chapters are readily available from craft stores or online. Angle cutters for wood are invaluable for cutting pieces to length and putting angles on the ends if required. Mainly we will be using a selection of small pieces of beech wood, which you can buy in packs or loose so you can buy exact quantities of a particular size. Don't try to use nails for very small pieces of wood as the wood will splinter and break along the grain, so make use of hot glue and/or waterproof wood glue. A roll of masking tape is handy for holding pieces in place while glue dries. Another good holding method is to use a small block of wood and a weight to hold pieces down.

Tile roof

Historically, once the technique of firing clay had evolved, mass production of tiles and bricks became common. Tiles then became a popular option for house roofs, particularly in areas with large natural deposits of clay. The tiles for this bird house project are made from craft sticks, which emulate clay tiles. Craft sticks look like short tongue depressors, or wide lollipop/popsicle sticks, with rounded ends. Packs of craft sticks can be bought from craft stores or online.

Making and laying tiles

I chose 1in (25mm) wide by 2½in (63mm) long pieces of craft stick for the tiles. Using the angle cutters I cut them in half to make 1¼in (32mm) lengths. I calculated that I would need nearly 100 tiles to cover both sides of the roof so I cut 50 sticks in half to make up the numbers. There were a few too many, but as the sticks were inexpensive and quick to make it didn't matter having leftovers. Your sizes may well be different to mine due to different size sticks you can get, so calculate your tiles accordingly.

Mark halfway along the craft stick

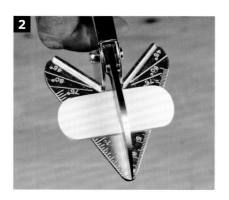

Place the stick in the angle cutter on its 90° line

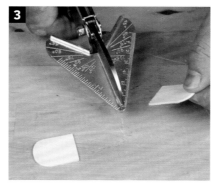

Cut the sticks in half to create two tiles

My calculations determined that I would need around 100 tiles

I chose the pitch roof to cover in tiles, but the curved or slant roof could just as easily be used. For tile roofs, I decided to use a mixture of glues and applied a line of waterproof wood glue along the top of the shingle and a blob of hot glue in the middle. The hot glue holds the tiles in place while the wood glue dries. The first row of tiles starts at the bottom of the roof and overhangs it by about ¼in (6mm). I then marked a line in the centre of the roof, followed by a line of marks up the roof to guide where to align the top of the tiles so they overlap the previous layer. My tiles were at about ¾in (19mm) apart.

To lay the tiles, start by gluing and positioning a tile either side of the centreline and continue laying the tiles until the outside edge of the roof is reached. You may have to cut the two outside tiles to fit. Start the next row from the centre again; this time the centre of the tile is in the centre of the roof. Continue laying on the tiles in this row until you reach the roof edge; trim the last two to width. Move onto the next row and follow the procedure as per the first two rows. This will get you almost to the top of the roof. Repeat the tile-laying process for the other side of the roof and, when complete, sand the edges of the end tiles flush with the roof.

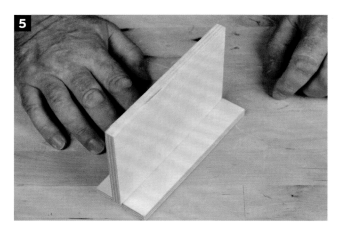

Make a simple jig by nailing two pieces of plywood at right angles to hold the roof pieces more-or-less horizontal to help when gluing on the tiles

Measure and mark the centre of the roof

Extend the line up the roof so it is easy to see when laying each row

At around ¾in (19mm) apart, mark lines to align the top of the tiles so the tiles overlap the previous row

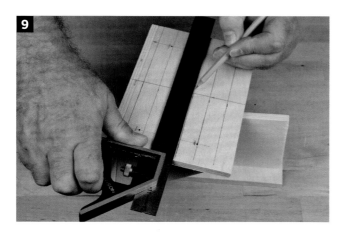

Extend the lines across the roof

Two types of glue are used for the roof: waterproof and hot glue

Apply two lines of waterproof glue on the roof ready for the first tile

Apply a line of hot glue on the middle of the tile. This quick drying glue will hold the tile in place until the waterproof glue dries

Glue tiles along the first row and mark the end tile so it can be cut

Cut the end tile and glue it in place

Repeat this on the other side of the roof

Glue the first tile of the second row in the centre of the roof

Glue all the second row tiles, lining up their tops along the line. Trim and glue the end tiles in place

Complete the tiling on this side...

...then turn the roof over and mark the other side

Complete the tiling on this side

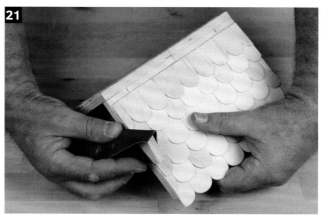

When the glue is completely dry, sand the edges of the tile flush with the roof

Cut a ridge piece from a piece of 90° 1in (25mm) corner moulding at about ½in (12mm) longer than the roof, then glue and lay it in place centrally on top of the tiles to cover their tops and overhang the roof by ¼in (6mm) front and back.

Finally, cut the trim boards from ⅜in (10mm) wide strips of beech; cut a 45° angle on one end and 90° on the other end. The angled ends fit under the ridge cap and the square ends line up with the last tile. Glue and nail the trim boards in place.

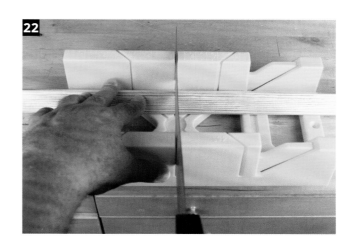

Cut the 90° angle to length

Apply glue to the roof for the ridge cap

Nail the ridge cap in place

Cut the 45° angle on the end of the trim boards

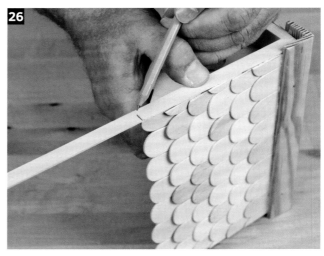

Mark and cut the trim boards to length

Glue and nail the trim boards in place

The finished tiled roof is ready for painting

Shingle roof

Shingles are simply thin slices of wood cut into tile-sized pieces. They are laid on the roof in layers so the bottom edge of one tile covers the top edge of another. They are also staggered so that their joins are over the mid-point of the tile beneath it. Shingles are also used as a wall covering and the process of applying them is the same as the roof. Start laying shingles at the bottom and work your way up the wall.

Making and laying shingles

The shingles for this roof are also made from craft sticks. The size I chose for the shingle roof was 1in (25mm) wide by 8in (200mm) long. I cut 1¼in (32mm) off both ends to remove the round ends, which were added to the ones on the tile roof. I cut 1½in (38mm) lengths from the remaining piece to give three shingles and calculated that I would need around 80 shingles in total.

I chose the curved roof to cover in shingles, but the pitch or slant roof could just as easily be used. For shingle roofs, apply a line of waterproof wood glue along the top of the shingle and a blob of hot glue in the middle. The hot glue holds the shingle in place while the wood glue dries.

Mark the craft sticks at lengths of 1½in (38mm) for each shingle

Place each stick in the angle cutter on the 90° line and cut them to length. You can use the curved ends to make tiles for the tiled roof

The first row of shingles starts at the bottom of the roof and overhangs it by about ¼in (6mm). Mark a line in the centre of the roof and then mark lines across the roof at spaces of around ¾in (19mm). This is to align the tops of the shingles to so they overlap the previous row.

Glue the first shingle and place it one side of the centreline, overhanging the roof by about ¼in

(6mm). Glue the next shingle and place it next to the first one. Continue laying the shingles until the outside edge of the roof is reached; you may have to cut the two outside tiles to fit. Start the next row from the centre again and align with the next line up. Glue and lay the first shingle so its mid-point is over the join of the two shingles below it. Continue laying on the shingles in this row until you reach the roof edge, then trim the last two to width.

Place the roof on the jig and mark the centre of the roof, then extend the line over the roof. I did this freehand, joining a few marks together. Now mark the position for the top of the first row of shingles then extend the line across the roof using a rule

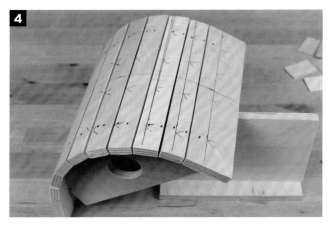

Mark lines for all the tops of the shingles at around ¾in (19mm) apart and get ready to shingle the roof

Run two lines of waterproof glue along the shingle

Apply a blob of hot glue on the roof and place the first two shingles either side of the centreline and aligned with the top line

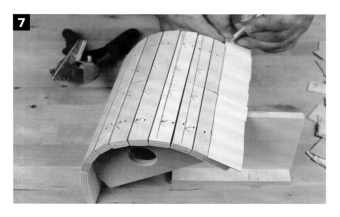

7

Continue gluing and placing the full shingles on the roof, then cut the two end shingles and glue them in place

Move onto the next two rows and follow the same procedure as for the first two. This should get you almost to the top of the roof. Repeat the whole process for the other side of the roof and then cut a ridge piece from the same sticks as the shingles. This time make it the whole length of the roof, then glue and lay it in place centrally on top of the shingles to cover their tops. Finish by sanding the edges of the end shingles flush with the roof.

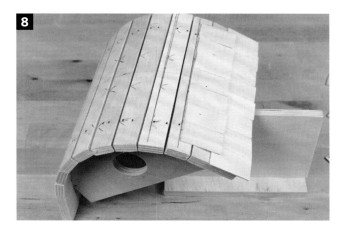

8

Lay the second row of shingles, but this time place the centre of the first shingle on the centreline of the roof so the shingles overlap

9

Repeat the process until this side of the roof is covered in shingles

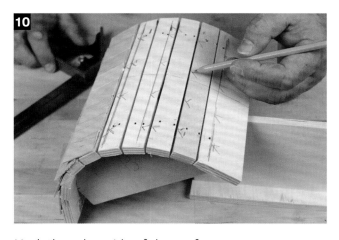

10

Mark the other side of the roof

11

Repeat the shingle laying process and cover this side of the roof with shingles

Sand the edges of the end shingles so they are flush with the roof

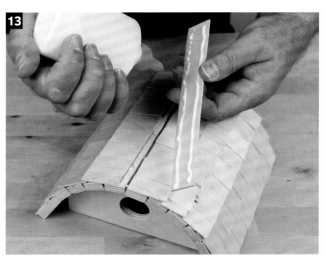

The ridge cap is made by cutting the round ends off one long craft stick. Apply two lines of glue to stick it to the shingles

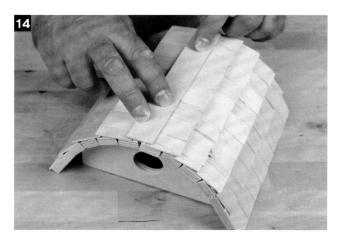

The ridge cap is in place and held until the glue has dried

Making the trim boards for the curved roof is a little more complicated than making them for straight roofs. I laid the end of the roof on a wide piece of beech from the wood pack and marked the high points of the shingles on it, then joined the marks freehand with a curved line. I calculated that I wanted the trim to be ⅜mm (10mm) wide and drew a curved line this distance away from, and inside, the first line. You need to cut the board out and, using the first one, copy it and cut three more to make four. Two trim boards are used on each end of the roof, so I lined up two boards on the roof end and overlapped their ends. Mark a vertical line at the midpoint of the roof on the top board then cut it. Lay the first piece on top of the second piece then mark and cut it; this will be the join. Cut the ends of the two pieces at the lower end of the roof. Repeat this for the two boards for the other end of the roof. Now glue and nail the trim boards in place and the roof is ready to paint or stain.

Lay the roof on top of a wide piece of wood to mark out the trim pieces. Mark dots at the high points to form a curve

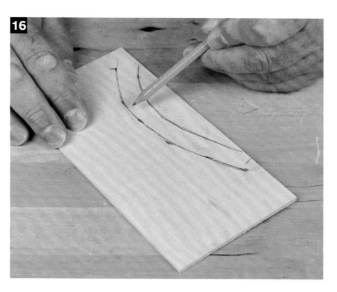

Create a freehand curved line between the dots, then draw another curved line around ⅜in (10mm) inside the first line

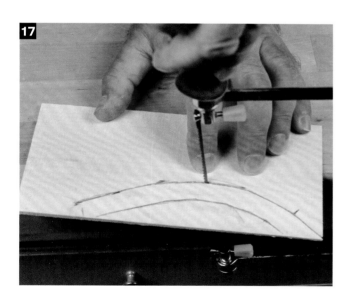

Saw the trim piece out. I used a coping saw, but if you have one you could use a scrollsaw

Create a freehand curved line between the dots, then draw another curved line around ⅜in (10mm) inside the first line

Lay two of the trim pieces on the end of the roof so the ends overlap, then mark a vertical line in the centre of the roof. Cut the end off the first trim piece and lay it on top of the second trim piece and mark its end

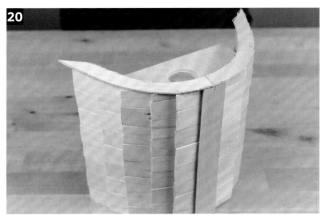

Cut the end of the second trim piece and the two pieces should butt together

Mark and cut all the trim pieces to length

Sand the curve to make it smooth

Glue and nail the trim pieces on the roof ends

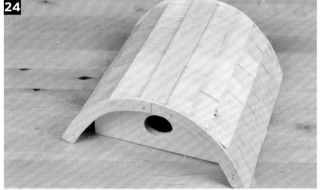

The roof is covered in shingles ready for its finish of paint or stain

Tin roof

Tin roofs are popular on barns and some homes in the USA. They are a very long-lasting roof covering, but can be quite expensive. I am not going to use metal for the roof, but make the roof from beech wood and paint it so that it resembles a tin roof.

Making and applying a tin roof

The pieces of wood used to emulate a tin roof effect are a ¾in (19mm) 90° corner moulding for the ridge cap and ⅛in (3mm) wide strips of beech from the craft store wood pack, to create the joins in the tin roof. I chose the pitch roof for this treatment, but it would look just as good on the curved and slant roofs. The curved roof would require the strips to be taped in place while the glue dries.

The first job is to cut the ridge cap from the ¾in (19mm) 90° corner moulding and make it slightly longer than the roof to allow for the trim boards. Glue it centrally on the roof so it overhangs either end. To hold it in place, pop a few nails in it for good measure. Then cut ten of the ⅛in (3mm) wide strips so they butt up to the ridge cap and are flush with the edge of the roof. Mark five lines vertically on the roof on both sides and equally spaced across the roof. Glue the strips centrally on these lines and when the glue is dry the roof needs the trim boards to be fitted.

You will need an angle piece and strips of wood to create the 'tin' roof

Mark the ridge cap just over the length of the roof to allow for the trim boards

Cut the ridge cap to length using a mitre box to ensure square ends

Sand the ends to make them smooth

Glue and nail the ridge cap in place centrally on the roof

Mark thin strips of wood to length so they butt up under the ridge cap and are flush with the lower roof edge

Using the angle cutters at 90°, cut ten of the strips, five for each side

Make five equally spaced marks along each side of the roof and...

…extend the lines using a square

Place the roof on the jig to hold it in a position that makes it easier to work on

Run a line of glue along the strips

Lay the first strip centrally on the line on the roof

Add each strip in turn, making sure the glue holds before moving onto the next

Complete the first side of the roof by adding all the strips of wood

Turn the roof over and mark this side ready for the strips of wood

Add the strips…

…one by one…

…until the side is complete

With the last strip of the tin roof in place, the roof is ready for the trim boards to be added

Cut the trim boards from ⅜in (10mm) wide strips, cut a 45° angle on one end and 90° on the other end. The angled ends fit under the ridge cap and the square ends line up with the lower roof end. Glue and nail the trim boards in place. After being painted the tin roof look will be complete.

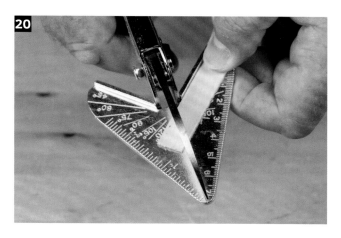

Use the angle cutters to cut 45° angles on the ends of four trim boards

Mark the trim boards flush with the lower end of the roof

Cut them at the 90° setting on the angle cutters

Glue and nail the trim boards in place

The finished tin roof ready to be painted

Thatch roof

Thatching is the craft of laying a roof with materials such as straw, water reed or rushes. The roof material is layered tightly to make it waterproof. Laying a thatch roof is a highly skilled job so I have come up with a simple way of creating the look of the thatch roof here. After experimenting with dried grass and reeds, I eventually came up with the idea of using bamboo sushi rolling/place mats to make the thatch roof.

Making and laying the thatch roof

The bamboo looks quite like straw and the mats are nicely stitched together so all the straws line up neatly – as if thatched by an expert! The bamboo mats are easy to get hold of and are very inexpensive. I bought a set of four mats online, which was useful as through experimenting I used more then I needed to.

My idea initially was to cut the mat to the width of one side of the pitch roof, and then the mat would have been long enough to get two pieces from that strip and one for the other side, too. However, as soon as you cut the threads holding the bamboo, all the pieces of bamboo fall apart and you end up with a pile of useless bamboo pieces. I then decided to cut two strips off the bamboo mat, retaining the end stitching that holds them together, then glue one strip on one side of the roof and one strip the other. The overhang is huge but I managed to roll them down so they didn't get in the way of each other.

Bamboo sushi rolling/place mats and corner moulding make up the thatch roof

Place the roof on the bamboo mat and draw a line along its width

Continue the line along the mat

Finish the line at the other end of the mat

Mark the line on both sides of the mat and cut along the line

Cut the next line...

...and you will have the two strips needed for the thatched roof

My previous idea of cutting the mat to length before gluing proved to be a disaster when the mat fell apart

Before gluing, slide the mat down the roof to give a ¼in (6mm) overhang at the bottom edge. The gap at the top will be covered with the ridge cap. The secret is to also glue the mat around the edges of the roof. You can use plenty of glue as it goes clear when it is dry. I found that a few office clips were perfect for holding everything in place while the glue dried.

Slide the mat down the roof by ¼in (6mm) to give an overhang as you would have on a thatched roof

Apply plenty of glue on the roof and along its edges

Roll the mat around one end of the roof and attach an office clip to hold it in place

Smooth the mat over the roof and roll it around the other end and attach a clip there, too

Glue the other side of the roof

Roll the mat around the end and clip in place

Smooth the mat over the roof and clip the end in place, too. Notice the large overhang of the mat

When the glue has dried, the ends of the mat can be trimmed to length along the bottom edge of the roof end. The bamboo strips will now be firmly attached. You can finish off the roof with a ridge cap made of ¾in (19mm) corner 90° angle moulding cut ½in (12mm) longer than the roof so there is a ¼in (6mm) overhang at each end.

When the glue is dry, use a sharp knife to cut the mat's stitches at the bottom edge of the roof end

Gently pull the end of the mat off the roof; there may be some excess glue holding it

The end piece of mat will come away and leave a nicely rolled edge on the roof

Repeat the process on all the roof edges

Cut the angle moulding to length for the ridge cap

Run two lines of glue along the underside of the ridge cap

Position the ridge cap on the roof and nail in place

The finished thatch roof is ready for sealing

Grass roof

Grass roofs are popular with environmentalists and for good reason. They provide splendid cover and insulation for a roof, as well as helping the planet by releasing oxygen into the atmosphere. On top of this the green of the grass blends nicely into a countryside location.

Installing the grass roof

The grass roof in this case is a piece of moss that looks like grass. Small pieces of this moss are available in craft stores. I used a piece about 12in (305mm) square. The first thing to do is to cut the piece of moss to fit the roof. I used the factory cut square edge as the starting point and cut the other two edges to the size of the roof.

A piece of moss, black plastic and wood strips are needed for the grass roof

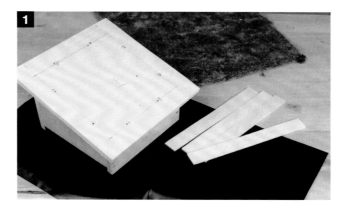

Using the factory-cut edges as a starting point, cut the moss the same size as the roof

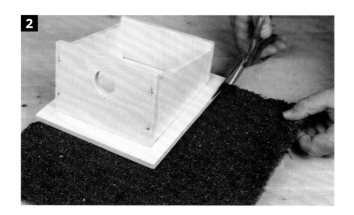

Tidy up the cut-away from the roof

Place the moss to one side and then cut some black plastic large enough so it wraps around the edge of the roof, around ¾in (19mm) larger in each direction. This will be used to create a waterproof barrier. You can use any kind of reasonable thick plastic for this; a bin liner perhaps. I used a sheet of black sticky-back plastic, which made the job easier as it held itself in place. Wrap the plastic around the edges of the roof, fold the corners, staple it in place and trim off any excess.

Cut a piece of black sticky-back plastic around ¾in (19mm) larger than the roof in each direction

Place the plastic on the roof, fold the edges and staple it in place

To tidy up the edges of the roof I cut pieces of ¾in (19mm) wide beech to the lengths of the roof edges and nailed them in place to create a retaining wall. On the back roof edge, drill a few holes in it to allow any rainwater to flow out and not sit in the roof tray. Lay the grass/moss in place and place a few large blobs of glue around its perimeter to stop the moss/grass blowing out.

Cut the roof trim pieces to length using the angle cutters at 90°

Drill holes in the back trim piece to allow water to drain from the roof

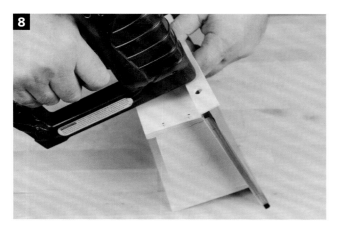

Glue and nail the trim pieces on the edges of the roof, back and front first…

…then the sides

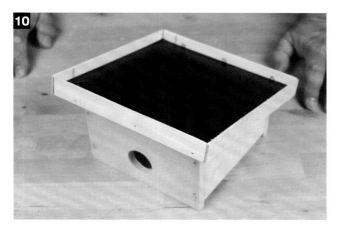

When the trim pieces are in place it makes a nice tray for the moss

Place some large blobs of glue around the perimeter of the roof to hold the moss in place when it is dropped into the tray

The completed grass roof, ready for finishing

Solar roof

This roof treatment is a bit on the adventurous side as it utilizes modern technology and solar power. The solar panel gathers energy from the sun and converts it into electrical power. In a full-size house the electricity is most likely to be used to power the house or pool but in our case, we are adding a luxury for the birds by providing them with a remote birdbath including a fountain pump powered by the solar panel. This does mean the fountain function is only available when it is sunny, but the birds can bathe any time.

Installing a solar roof

The first thing to do is to buy the solar panel, fountain pump and birdbath. I found what I wanted at an online store. The 5¼ x 5¾in (132 x 145mm) solar panel was just a bit smaller than the roof, so I needed to make some infill pieces to tidy it up.

Before creating the infill pieces, it is a good idea to lay a waterproof barrier of black plastic on the roof and hold it in place with staples in the roof edges.

A piece of bin liner will work, but I was able to use black sticky-back plastic. Cut some 1⅛in (30mm) wide wood trim pieces the same length as the roof edges and nail them in place so they sit above the roof to create a tray and tidy up the roof edges. Drill holes in the back piece to let any rainwater out and cut one of them larger to allow the plug of the fountain pump wire to pass through and connect to the solar panel.

You will need beech strips, a sheet of black plastic, wooden corner moulding and a solar fountain kit to complete the roof

Mark the sticky-back plastic around ¾in (19mm) larger than the roof in each direction so it will wrap around the roof edge

Cut it to size

Cut lengths of 1⅛in (30mm) wide wood trim boards to fit the roof

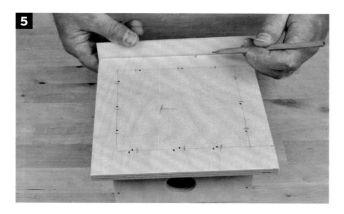

Mark the back trim board where it needs to drain and where cable holes will be drilled

Also mark the height of the holes so that the bottom of the hole is just below the surface of the roof

Drill the holes using a piece of wood under the workpiece to protect the bench

Drill all three holes the same size...

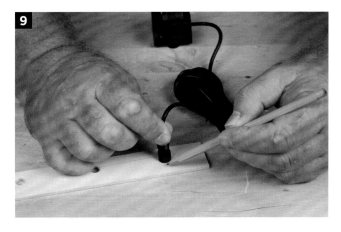

...then mark round the fountain pump plug on the end hole...

...and file the hole larger...

...so the plug fits through it

Place the black plastic on the roof and fold the edges and corners and staple it in place

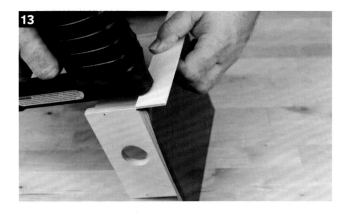

Nail the edge trim boards on the sides of the roof...

...then nail on the front and back trim boards

For the infill pieces, the ¾in (19mm) corner angle moulding I had was perfect for the job. You need to cut this to length and also cut a notch out in the rear piece to allow the cable to pass through it. The side pieces also need a small cut made on their ends so they fit over the trim boards. To cut them, an inexpensive mitre box will be all you need, apart from a relatively fine tooth saw.

Cut the four pieces and glue them in place. The solar panel will just sit in the tray you have created. My panel also needed a small block under one end to hold it up. Lastly, thread the wire for the fountain pump through the back and decide where the birdbath will go. I am going to attach it to a bird house base, but you can clamp the birdbath onto anything you want.

Cut the first angle piece to length

The mitre box is great for accurate square cuts

Mark the thickness of the trim boards on the angle pieces of wood

Cut to this line on both ends, making sure not to cut through the top and create a step

Place the angles in place on both sides of the trim board to make sure they fit

Mark the front and back pieces and cut to length

Cut a notch in the back angle piece for the solar panel's cable to pass through and check this fits

Run a line of glue along the top of the trim board

Place the first angle piece in position and then glue along the top of the next trim board

Place the angle on the top of the trim board and continue adding them until finished

Pass the plug of the fountain pump cable through the hole and cut out

Attach the plug to the solar panel and then place the panel in the roof recess. I needed a small block under one end of the panel to keep it level

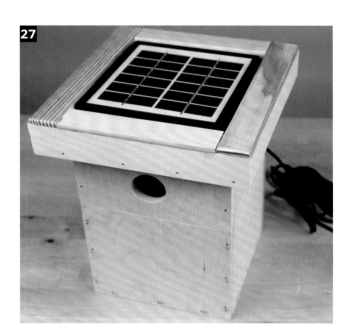

The solar roof in place on top of the base box shows the fountainhead and long cable

The rear view shows the solar panel cable passing through the hole in the trim board

Solar panel base addition

An additional attachment to go on the base is the birdbath with solar-powered fountain. This can be attached directly to the bottom of the bird house, but it can also be attached to the bottom of the decorative base too.

The birdbath and bracket alongside the plywood piece for its mount

Mark out where the birdbath clamp will come to on its plywood mounting plate

Mark the holes for screwing the plate to the base

Drill the holes in the plate. Use a block of wood to protect the bench

Screw the plate to the underside of the bird house

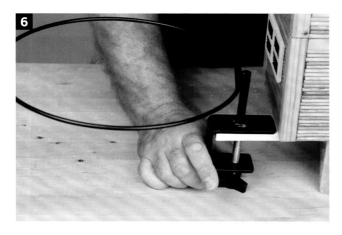

Clamp the birdbath bracket to the mounting plate

Place the fountain in the birdbath. Feed the cable through the hole in the roof and connect it to the solar panel

The studio lights were bright enough to power the fountain

The bird house in its natural environment, waiting for some sunshine to power the fountain

Wall treatments

BIRD HOUSES CAN BE MADE MUCH MORE ATTRACTIVE BY USING WALL TREATMENTS COPIED FROM FULL-SIZED HOUSES. THE OPTIONS ARE MANY AND VARIED. THE ONES I HAVE CHOSEN ARE THE TYPES THAT WILL MAKE THE BIRD HOUSES MOST APPEALING... IF ONLY TO THE HUMAN OWNERS RATHER THAN THE FEATHERED OCCUPANTS!

What you need

- Angle cutters
- Saw
- Waterproof wood glue
- Hot glue gun with glue
- Hammer and nails or nail gun and nails (various sizes)
- Pencil
- Sharp knife
- 100 grit sandpaper (and wooden block)
- Wood file
- Tape measure

- Ruler
- Masking tape
- Combination square
- Saws
- Mitre box
- Drill
- Screwdriver
- Clips
- Relevant wood and materials for each wall treatment

Horizontal siding

Horizontal siding is a popular wall treatment on many styles of house and it can be mixed with any of our roof options. Painting it with a contrasting trim colour will make the bird house look extremely eye-catching. I chose to show this wall treatment with a slant roof, which might be typical of a modern town abode in a chic neighbourhood. I used small packs of beech wood to make the siding, which are readily available from a craft store.

Making and applying the horizontal siding

The first step in this process is to apply the corner moulding to all four corners of the basic box. The angle moulding not only hides the edge of the plywood, it also makes it easy to apply the siding as the pieces just need cutting to length and no mitres are required. The edge moulding is a ⁹⁄₁₆in (15mm) wood angle, cut to the length of the side height, then glued and nailed on. I made them the same length as the sides of the bird house, which creates a recess that the top will locate into. I used waterproof glue and shorter ⁹⁄₁₆in (15mm) pins in the nail gun as they are long enough to do the job.

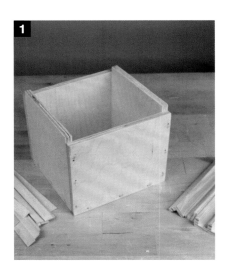

The basic box, corner moulding and strips of wood are needed to make the horizontal siding

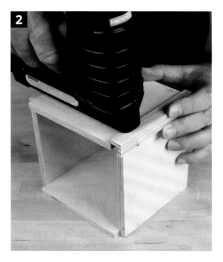

Cut the moulding to length then glue and nail in place

Do the same on all the corners of the box

In the pack of beech wood I found numerous pieces of ⅜in (10mm) wide by ⁵⁄₆₄in (2mm) thick boards, around 4in (100mm) long. These are ideal for the siding and just need cutting to length and an angle sanded on their edges to give them the look of a V-jointed board when placed next to each other. The first thing to do is to cut the ⅜in (10mm) wide strips that will cover the join between the roof and box. Mark and cut them to length between the corner angles, then place them on the front and rear, aligned with the top of the corner angle and draw a line across the box. Repeat this process on the back. This strip will be glued to the roof to hide the join between the roof and box.

The uppermost siding piece on the base box should be glued and placed so its edge is against the line drawn. This is to allow the siding that will be applied to the roof to be set down to hide the join when the roof is fitted to the base. Continue gluing and placing the siding pieces until the bottom of the box is reached. It is likely it will overhang and this excess will be cut off when the glue is dry.

There may be a tendency for the pieces to move or curl, but this can be prevented. Simply cut a piece of wood and place it on top of the siding, then put the weight on it, which will hold the siding pieces down while the glue dries. When the glue is dry on the first face, turn the house round and repeat the process on all the faces. The last thing to do is to trim off the excess width of the siding strips with a sharp knife and sand smooth.

Mark the first piece of siding the same length as the distance between the corner angles

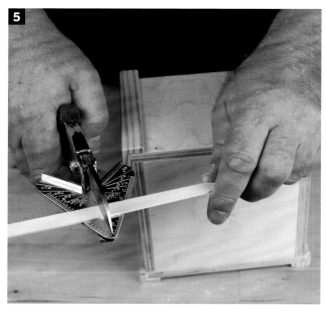

Cut it using the 90° marks on the angle cutters

Align the top edge of the siding piece with the top edge of the corner moulding and draw a line across the front of the box. This line will be the start line for the first piece of siding. The rest of the siding pieces will be laid below

Sand the edges of the siding pieces so a chamfer runs along its length on both sides. When butted to the next piece it will look like a V-joint

Glue along the length of the first piece of siding

Then position it under the line you previously drew

Continue laying pieces of siding until the bottom is reached. The last piece will be trimmed to width

A pad made up of a piece of wood and a weight will hold them in place until the glue dries

Repeat the process on the back and on the sides. The last piece is likely to overhang the bottom and will need trimming off

Use a sharp knife to score a line on the siding and cut off the excess on the last piece of wood

Use sandpaper and a block to sand the siding flush with the underside of the box

The siding can now be applied to the roof chosen for this house. It will be the same process as for the base with the slant or flat roof, including the corner moulding. The pitch and curved roofs will not need the corner moulding.

Apply the four angle corner pieces, then fill in between them with the siding pieces until the top is reached. Don't worry that the hole is covered up as this is cut out again with a knife and sanded round. The top of the siding will have to have an angle cut on it to match the angle of the roof.

When the roof is completed, you can drill holes in the front and rear corners so that the top can be fixed to the base with screws. The screws can easily be removed again at the end of the season for cleaning, or even for a change of roof style.

Place the roof on top of the base box and mark the corner angle to length

Cut, glue and nail all the corner pieces on the roof

Place the roof back on the box, glue the top half of the siding piece and butt it up to the top siding piece on the box. This will overlap the join and help avoid water getting into the bird house

Continue laying the siding up the front of the roof. Cover the hole as this will be cut out again later

Finish the front then...

...repeat the process on the sides

On the slant roof mark the slant angle on the siding...

...and cut the angle

Continue to the top of the roof

Mark the position of the hole

Use a sharp knife to rough cut the siding around the inside of the hole

Roll up sandpaper and sand the hole smooth

Drill holes where screws will hold the two pieces of the bird house together

The finished siding treatment using the flat roof. Any of the other roof shapes could be used instead

Vertical metal siding

The vertical metal siding wall treatment is reminiscent of industrial and agricultural buildings such as factories or barns. We are not going to use metal for the siding, but wood strips to create the effect of the metal siding. The strips of beech wood are from the pack I bought at the craft store. When painted the wood will look almost like the real thing. Your choice of roof may differ from mine and any of the roof styles will be suitable.

Making and applying the vertical metal siding

This wall treatment begins with adding the corner moulding to all four corners of the base box. The pieces are cut to length and glued and nailed in place. I used the waterproof glue for this and used shorter ⁹⁄₁₆in (15mm) pins in the nail gun. I made the vertical pieces the same length as the sides of the bird house. This also creates a recess that the top will locate into.

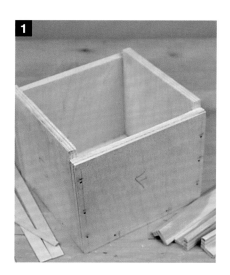

Corner angle and wood strips are needed to make the vertical metal siding

Cut the corner angle to the length of the side's height, then glue and nail it in place

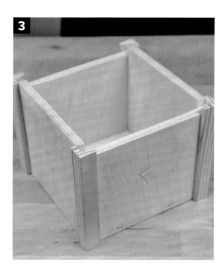

Do this for all the corners

The next thing to do is to cut the ⅜in (10mm) wide strips that will cover the join between the roof and box. Mark and cut it to length between the corner angles, then place it on the front aligned with the top of the corner angle and draw a line across the box. Repeat this process on the back. This strip will be glued to the roof to hide the join between the roof and box.

Mark a strip of wood the length of the distance between the corner angles

Cut the strip of wood to length using the 90° angle on the angle cutters

Use the piece to mark a line across the front of the box. Its top lines up the top of the angle moulding

The beech pieces I chose from the pack are ⅜in (10mm) wide by ⁵⁄₆₄in (2mm) thick. I started on the front of the box with the box laid on its back. Cut the strips to length, starting from the bottom of the box to the line you have just drawn. I needed seven strips on each wall and started by gluing one to butt against the corner moulding and flush with the bottom of the box. Next, use a spacer cut from a ³⁄₁₆in (4mm) wide strip placed against the first vertical strip and then glue the next vertical strip in place. Move the spacer strip to the side of the last vertical strip and repeat the process until

the wall is covered. The last vertical strip may need cutting to width to fit against the corner moulding. Use masking tape and make a plate. Use a weight on top of the siding to prevent the siding pieces curling up as the glue dries.

When the glue has dried turn the box onto its front and repeat the process. The side walls do not have the horizontal strip at the top, so cut the vertical pieces to the full height of the wall and glue them in place using the same technique.

Mark a strip of wood the distance between the line and the bottom of the box

Cut it to length and add others to make about 15 pieces. Glue the first piece…

…and place it on the box vertically, butting its edge to the corner angle

Use a thin strip as a spacer between the first vertical strip and the next

Continue with this until the last vertical piece is against the corner angle on the other side

The front is now finished onto the side

Mark the vertical piece the full length of the side

Cut the piece to length, plus about 15 others

Glue the piece and…

…place it on the box so that its edge butts against the corner angle

Use the spacer and continue gluing and placing the vertical pieces on the box until the corner angle on the other side is reached

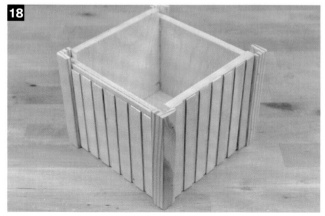

Complete all sides of the box

The roof I chose for this bird house is the curved roof, which I think looks more barnlike, but you can choose any roof you prefer. The horizontal piece needs to be cut to length and glued on first. The vertical pieces are cut to length above this horizontal part; I just cut them square at the top rather than trying to match the curve of the roof. This looks quite agricultural and is much easier to make. Glue them in line with the vertical pieces on the base box and go straight over the hole so you don't have to mess around with small, fiddly pieces. When the glue is dry, the hole can be cut in

the vertical siding pieces using a sharp knife and a file or sandpaper to make the hole smooth again. Repeat the process on the back wall of the roof but in this case, there is no need to consider the hole as there isn't one.

When the roof is completed, drill holes in the front and rear corners so that the top can be fixed to the base with screws. The screws can be easily removed again at the end of the season for cleaning, or even for a change of roof style.

Place the roof on the box and glue the top half of the horizontal strip. Stick this to the roof, butting onto the top of the vertical pieces

Mark and cut a vertical piece from the top of the inside of the roof to the top of the horizontal piece

Apply glue to the roof…

…and stick the pieces on it. It doesn't matter that the hole is covered as it will be cut out again later

Glue vertical pieces of wood until the sides of the roof are reached

Use a sharp knife to cut out the hole

Roll up sandpaper and sand the hole smooth

Mark the positions for the screw holes to attach the roof to the box

Drill holes where screws will hold the two pieces of the bird house together

The vertical metal siding is ready for painting

Tudor-style beams

Tudor-style houses were originally built as a wooden frame for the structure, with the gaps between filled in with wooden sticks and plaster. The style is still popular today, but the wooden beams are now fake pieces applied on top of the surface of the walls. The idea here is to try to recreate that look with pieces of wood applied to the surface of the walls. You can follow my design, or you can create your own version for other styles of Tudor beams. The beams are painted in a contrasting colour to give the building the effect of a Tudor house.

Making and applying the Tudor-style beams

Start the Tudor-style beams by adding the corner moulding to all four corners of the basic box. Cut the pieces to length and glue and nail them in place. I used the waterproof glue and the shorter 9/16in (15mm) pins in the nail gun. I made the beams the same length as the sides of the bird house, which creates a recess that the top will locate into. The next thing to do is to cut the 3/8in (10mm) wide strips that will cover the join between the roof and box. Mark and cut it to length between the corner angles, then place it on the front aligned with the top of the corner angle and draw a line across the box. Repeat this process on the back. This strip will be glued to the roof to hide the join between the roof and the box.

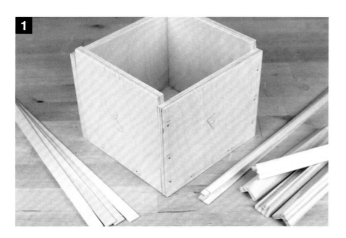

Wood strips and 90° corner angles are needed to create the Tudor effect

Mark the corner angle at the height of the box side

Cut and glue the corner angle then nail it in place flush with the box bottom and side top

Glue and nail all the corner angle pieces

Mark a strip of wood the distance between the corner angles

Cut the strip and place it between the corner angles and flush with their top and draw a line across the box

The first piece to apply is the ¼in (6mm) wide horizontal door frame piece. I made the inside of this 3¼in (85mm) high and the two vertical frame pieces 2in (50mm) apart in the centre of the wall. The doors (as described in the following chapter) are the same size, so the door you choose will just fit in place. Now cut three vertical pieces to fit between the door frame and the drawn line at the top of the box and glue them in place. Next, cut two short pieces with opposing 45° angles on their ends to fit diagonally between the corner moulding and the door frame at 45° and glue them in place. Lastly, cut and glue two pieces horizontally on top of the angle pieces and to the door frame.

Mark the height of the inside of the door frame at 3¼in (85mm) high…

…then 1in (25mm) apart in the centre of the wall. The door (to be made later) will be 3¼in (85mm) high x 2in (50mm) wide

Mark more lines, three vertically above the door and a couple either side of the door halfway up the frame. These are positions to place more frames

Mark then cut the frame so that it fits between the corner angles

Glue then stick it in place with its bottom edge on the pencil line

Mark, cut and glue three vertical pieces in place on the top row. Mark the length of the vertical door frames between the bottom edge of the top door frame and the bottom of the box. Glue them so their inside edges are on the vertical lines

Mark opposing 45° angles on either ends of a short strip. Cut them and glue the strip in place. Repeat on the other side

Mark and cut the horizontal pieces between the corner angle and the outside of the door frame. Glue it in place and repeat on the other side

Tudor house building was not a precise science, so any unevenness in positioning of the beams will give the bird house some period charm. The side walls have a horizontal beam at the same height as the front's door header beam and three vertical pieces above it, with a wide ⁹⁄₁₆in (15mm) strip horizontally placed above them. The lower part of the wall has a narrow horizontal beam at the same height as the front's mid-door piece, 2in (50mm) away from the top beam, and two vertical beams centred on the wall and at 2¼in (55mm) apart. As with the door, these are the dimensions of the windows described in the following chapter.

The last wall to treat is the back wall, and this has the horizontal beam placed at the same height as the front's door header beam and three short pieces placed vertically above it. These three pieces are cut ⅛in (3mm) short of the top of the wall to allow for the horizontal beam of the roof to butt up to them. A vertical beam is placed in the centre of the wall from the ground up to the horizontal beam. Two pieces are then cut with 45° ends and are placed diagonally either side of the central vertical beam.

Cut, glue and place two frame pieces: one 1½in (38mm) up and the other 2in (50mm) away from it

Cut and glue the two vertical frame pieces in place centrally on the wall at 2in (50mm) apart. The window is 2in (50mm) square and will fit inside the frame

Cut and glue three short strips to go vertically above the window

Next, cut and glue a horizontal strip on top of the three vertical strips. This lines up with the one on the front and back. Repeat the framing process on the other side of the box

The back of the box is similar to the front but without the door frame. I added a vertical strip in the centre flanked by strips at 45° on either side

Place the roof on top of the box and run a line of glue along the top of the previously cut strip. This will ensure it only adheres to the roof piece

The roof I chose for the Tudor house is the pitch roof with a thatch finish as this is more in keeping with the Tudor style than the other roofs. Glue and fit the horizontal beam; its length is cut at the distance between the corner pieces on the base box and it is glued on the gable end of the roof, protruding down to the line on the box to cover the join between the roof and box. On top of this, two diagonal beams will be placed, so cut a 45° angle on one end and a 90° on the other end. These beams will clear the hole on the gable end and look

like roof supports. Finally, cut 45° angles on each end or a short beam that goes over the hole and glue that in place. Repeat this beam pattern on the rear gable, too.

When the roof is completed, you can drill holes in the front and rear corners so that the top can be fixed to the base with screws. These screws are easily removed again at the end of the season for cleaning, or even for a change of roof style.

Place the strip on the roof piece and set down to the vertical strips on the box

Mark and cut 45° strips to go either side of the hole, then glue them in place

Cut one more strip to go above the hole. It has opposing 45° angles on either end. Glue and stick the strip in place

Repeat the process on the back

The drill holes where screws will hold the two pieces of the bird house together

The Tudor-style bird house is ready for painting

Log cabin

Log cabins are always a popular wall style to create in both full size on real houses as well as in miniature. Many dream of the seclusion of living in a log cabin and the outdoor lifestyle that goes with it. Birds may not have the same aspirations, but we can still enjoy watching them in their woodland home. The construction of a log cabin is a complex procedure and the ends of the logs are cut with a joint that locks them together. For our bird house, the logs don't need to lock together. Instead we will make a wall covering treatment to emulate the look of a log cabin.

Making and applying the logs

The logs that make up the cabin are made of ½in (12mm) dowel cut to two different lengths. The long pieces are 7¼in (185mm) long and the shorter pieces are 6in (150mm) long. Sand round the ends of the logs to give then a chamfer. The idea with this wall treatment is to get it to look like a log cabin with the log ends protruding past each other. However, instead of the logs interlocking at the ends they simply butt up to one another.

Instead of working on individual walls, the logs are applied all round from the bottom up. I found that using hot glue works well for this application as it dries quickly and holds the log in place. I then used the waterproof glue to run along the top of the hot glue line at the back of the log and filled in any gaps to make it water resistant. I then ran a line of waterproof glue along the top of the log to increase the holding power and water resistance.

Take a short log and run a thick line of hot glue along it then stick it to the bottom front of the base. Making sure it is flush with the walls on both ends, then continue with the waterproof glue technique. Glue and stick the long logs on the side walls, making sure they are protruding past the front logs front and back and then attach the base log on the back wall. Now take the short logs and glue them on the side walls and flush with the front and back. Next, glue the long logs to the front and rear walls, making sure their ends protrude past the side logs.

Continue this process all the way up the wall until you reach the top. As the wall height is divisible by the diameter of the log, this means the top log is flush with the top of the front wall.

Two different lengths of ½in (12mm) dowel are used to make the log cabin effect

Mark the width (6in/150mm) of a box side on a dowel and cut it to length. About 30 pieces of this length will be needed

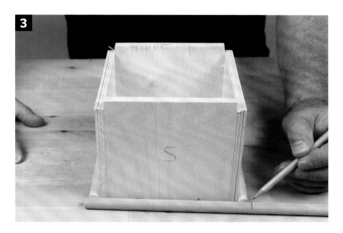

Place two pieces of dowel on either side of the box and mark a dowel slightly longer than the width of the box and the dowels. Mine was 7¼in (185mm) long. Around 30 of these pieces will be needed

Sand round the ends of the shorter logs to make them smooth. Sand deeper on the long logs to give them a chamfer on their ends

Apply a line of hot glue along the log...

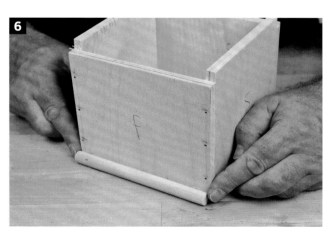

...then stick it on the base of the box on the front

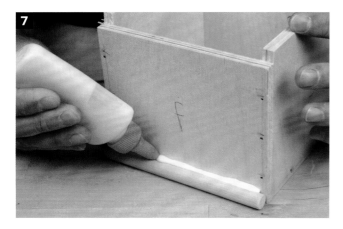

Run a large line of waterproof glue along the top of the log to fill gaps and make it water resistant

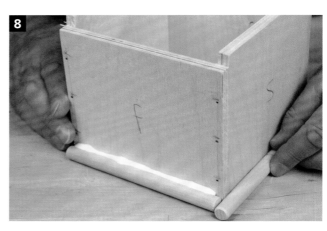

Hot glue the log on the side and make sure the front of the log protrudes past the front log

Repeat this on the other side

Run a bead of waterproof glue along the top of the layer of logs

Move onto the next layer and hot glue a short log, stick it to the side of the box and on top of the previous log

Now do the same with the front log, making sure it protrudes slightly past the side log

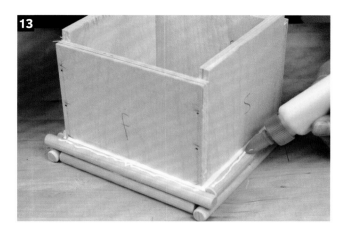

Repeat the waterproof gluing process…

…and continue to stick the logs all the way to the top of the box

The roof posed a new problem on the front as it would be difficult to cut the logs round the hole, as well as looking a bit odd with the short cut ends of the logs. I decided to make a hole plate from ½in (12mm) ply and first drilled the hole (the same diameter as the one in the roof piece), with the hole saw. I cut it 2in (50mm) high so its top would line up with the logs and 1⅞in (47mm) wide as this looked right.

Glue the hole plate to the roof end so the holes in the roof and plate line up then cut and glue short pieces of log that go around it. Now cut the logs and cover the rear roof end; this is much simpler as there is no hole. I cut square ends on the logs to make it easier and give it a rustic effect. Make sure that the two lower pieces are cut short to expose the wall as this is where the screws to hold the roof will be positioned. With the roof fixed to the base with screws, the screws can easily be removed again at the end of the season for cleaning, or even for a change of roof style.

Place the roof on top of the box and using a small piece of plywood…

…mark on the gable end the position of the top log

Measure up from this mark for the centre of the hole

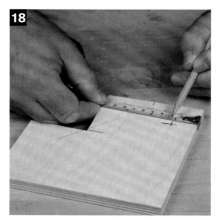

Select a piece of ⅜in (10mm) thick plywood for the hole plate. Mark the centre of the hole

Use four pieces of log to mark the vertical size of the plate

Use the hole saw to cut the hole in the plywood. Be careful to hold the work in a vice while doing this. The reason it is cut to size in the next step is so that there is wood to hold in the vice now

Now saw the plate to size

Glue and position the hole plate on the line where the top log finishes

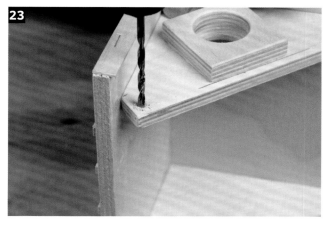

Drill holes where screws will hold the two pieces of the bird house together

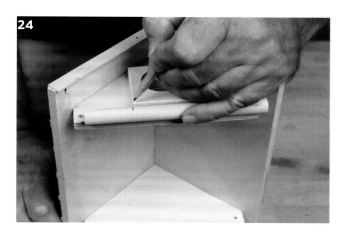

Mark a log to fit between the screw hole and hole plate. Make sure there is still enough room for a screwdriver for when you need to open the box

Cut and glue the log in place

Repeat on the other side of the plate. The next layer uses logs the same length

Cut more logs and finish at the top

Repeat on the back of the bird house. This time there is no hole to worry about

The finished log cabin effect, ready for painting

Brick walls

Traditional brick houses are found all over the world. The size and colour of bricks may vary, but the building process is the same for all. Bricks are placed side by side in a line, held together with mortar. Another line of bricks is placed on top of that line, but offset by half a brick. This ensures that the bricks interlock – and the process continues until the wall reaches the height desired. As this process would be far too time-consuming for our bird house, I am going to create the effect of bricks using strips of wood with a surface treatment.

Making and applying the bricks

Start by adding the corner moulding to all four corners of the basic box. The pieces are cut to length and glued and nailed in place. I used the waterproof glue for this and put shorter ⁹⁄₁₆in (15mm) pins in the nail gun as they are long enough to do the job. Now cut the ⅜in (10mm) wide strips that will cover the join between the roof and box.

Mark and cut a strip the length of the distance between the corner angles, then place it on the front aligned with the top of the corner angle and draw a line across the box. Repeat this process on the back. This strip will be glued to the roof to hide the join between the roof and box.

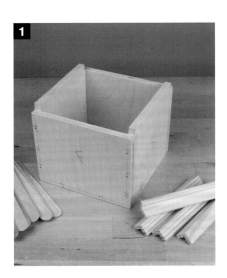

You will need craft sticks and angle mouldings to create the brick wall effect

Cut the corner angle to the same length as the box sides then glue and nail in place

Mark a ⅜in (10mm) strip of wood the same length as the distance between the corner angles

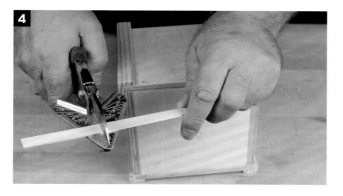

Cut it using the 90° angle on the angle cutters

Align the top edge of the piece with the top edge of the corner moulding and draw a line across the front of the box. This line will be the start line for the first piece of brick. The rest of the siding pieces will be laid below. Add one on the back, too

Instead of using clay bricks I am going to use ½in (12mm) wide craft sticks purchased from the craft store. Lay the base box on its back and cut enough strips to cover the wall between the corner mouldings. I cut around 40 to cover the whole house. The strips now need crafting to make them look like bricks. This is done by sanding a chamfer all around their edges then filing vertical lines in them 1in (25mm) apart, which will make them look like individual bricks.

I made a little template jig, which is just a piece of wood with pencil marks on it. Place a strip on the jig and mark the end and this will be where alternate strips will line up to. Then, working from

the centre of the strip, mark lines on the jig 1in (25mm) apart until the ends are reached. Now move the strip ½in (12mm) to the right and mark its end on the jig. This is where the other alternate pieces will be lined up to. Place the first strip on the jig and mark lines on it from the position of the lines on the jig then do this on half of the pieces. Now line up a strip on the next end line and mark lines on the rest of the strips. Using a square file, file V-grooves in the faces of the strips on lines you have marked. You can start gluing the strips to the wall, making sure that you use alternate pieces to give the offset look that brick walls have. Continue this process on all the walls.

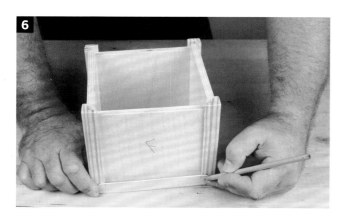

Mark a ½in (12mm) wide craft stick the distance between the corner angles

Cut the craft stick to length using the 90° angle on the angle cutters

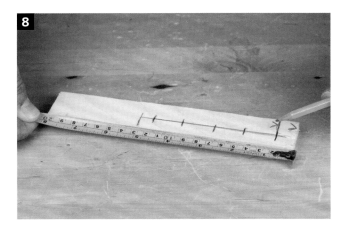

Make a jig to mark the strips. Use a piece of ply for this and mark it for the size of bricks

With a stick aligned to the first line on the jig, strips can be marked for a row of bricks

With the stick aligned on the end of the jig, mark the offset for the next row of bricks

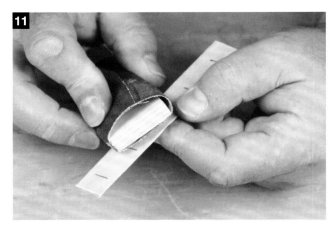

Use sandpaper on a block to sand a chamfer along the edges of the strip

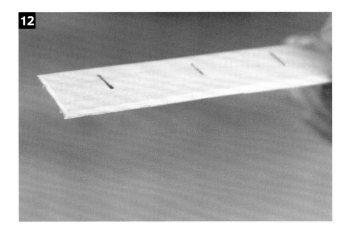

The chamfers, when butted together, will give the appearance of a cement line

Using a square file create a V-groove on the strip on each marked brick line

The V-groove will give the appearance of a cement line between the bricks

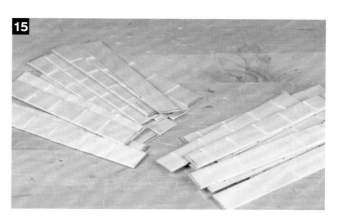

Cut enough strips to cover the house. Make half of them one way and the other half the other way

Glue the first strip of bricks and lay it against the top line drawn earlier

Using an alternate strip of bricks, glue and place it below the first one, then continue adding alternate strips until the bottom of the box is reached. The last strip will probably overhang and this will be cut flush when the glue dries

Cover the side with alternate strips, and if needed, place a wood pad and weight to hold the strips while the glue dries

Use a sharp knife to score the brick strips that overhang the bottom and cut them off...

20

...and sand them flush with the bottom of the box

Cover the walls using the same technique, but cut the ends of the brick strips to match the roof angle or curve. On the end with the hole, just cover it up. It is easier to do this rather than trying to cut small pieces around it. When the glue is dry, cut onto the strips covering the hole and sand them round flush with the hole in the wall end.

When the roof is complete you can drill holes in the front and rear corners so that the top can be fixed to the base with screws. The screws are easily removed again at the end of the season for cleaning, or even for a change of roof style.

21

Place the roof on the box and glue the top of the joining strip cut earlier. Glue it to the roof only

22

Cut a brick strip, leaving it short of the roof ends to allow for the screw holes to hold the roof to the box. Glue this to the roof

23

Cut angles on the ends of the brick strips to allow for the pitch of the roof

24

Stick the brick strips all the way up the roof. Don't worry about covering the hole as this will be cut out again later

Mark the extent of the hole

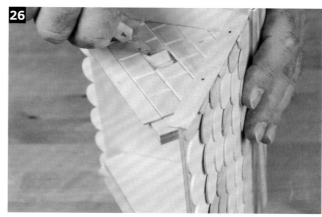

Use a sharp knife to cut out the hole

Roll up sandpaper and sand the hole smooth

Mark the position of the holes for the screws that will hold the roof onto the box

Drill all four screw holes

The brick wall treatment is now ready for painting

Bamboo walls

Bamboo is an extremely popular material for building as it has excellent strength qualities. Bamboo also grows quickly so is eminently renewable. It is commonly used as a wall treatment in Japan, but is being seen more in the West as people use more eco-friendly materials. It is not possible to get bamboo in small scale for the bird house so I found ³⁄₃₂in (4mm) diameter dowel, which will create a respectable emulation of bamboo.

Making and applying the bamboo

Start by adding the corner moulding to all four corners of the basic box. The pieces are cut to length and glued and nailed in place. I used the waterproof glue for this and put shorter ⁹⁄₁₆in (15mm) pins in the nail gun as they are long enough to do the job. The next thing to do is to cut the ³⁄₈in (10mm) wide strips that will cover the join between the roof and box. Mark and cut it to length between the corner angles, then place it on the front aligned with the top of the corner angle and draw a line across the box. Repeat this process on the back. This strip will be glued to the roof to hide the join between the roof and the box.

You will need small diameter dowels to fit between the corner angles to create the bamboo effect

Cut the corner angle to the same length as the box sides then glue and nail it in place

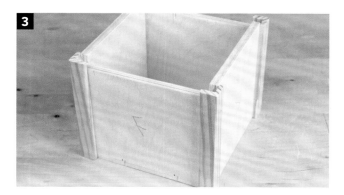

Do the same with all four corners

Cut a ⅜in (10mm) wood strip to the length between the corner angles, place it flush with the top of the side and mark a line across the front. Do the same on the back. This piece will be glued to the roof to cover the gap between the roof and the box

The bamboo is a ³⁄₃₂in (4mm) diameter dowel, cut to fit between the corner angles. Cut around 140 pieces to cover the walls and roof. First, run lines of glue all over the wall, then using a homemade glue comb, spread the glue to create a large area of contact for the dowels to adhere to. The first piece of dowel on the front is laid in alignment with the line drawn for the gap-covering strip. Keep laying the dowel next to each other until the bottom of

the box is reached. The last piece may not be flush with the bottom of the box but can be sanded flush when the glue is dry.

Turn the box round and repeat the process, but this time start from the bottom and work up. It doesn't matter if the last piece does not line up at the top as it will be covered by the roof. Repeat the process on the back and other side.

Take a piece of dowel and mark it the length between the corner angles

Cut it to length. You will need to make about 140 pieces to cover the house

Cut a small strip of wood and file V-notches in it. This is going to be a glue comb

Run lines of glue across the front…

…then use the comb to spread out the glue

From the top line place pieces of dowel…

…and work towards the bottom. The last piece might be flush with the bottom, but if not it will be sanded flush later

It is a good idea to use a pad and weight to hold the pieces in place while the glue dries

Move round to the side and repeat the process. This time, start at the bottom though

Continue laying on the dowels until the top is reached. It doesn't matter if it is not flush

Place the chosen roof on the box. I chose the flat roof with a solar panel as I thought it fitted in well with the eco-theme of the bamboo house. However, you can choose any roof you like. Cut, glue and nail on the corner angles and then spread glue along the top of the gap-covering strip and stick it to the roof. Spread glue over the roof end and start laying down the dowels from the gap-covering strip up. The dowels will cover the hole, but this will be cut out again later. Repeat the dowel-laying process

on the sides and back and when the glue is dry, cut out the hole in the front and sand smooth with rolled-up sandpaper.

When the roof is complete you can drill holes in the front and rear corners so that the top can be fixed to the base with screws. This can be easily removed again at the end of the season for cleaning, or even for a change of roof style.

Glue and place the join-covering strip above the top piece of dowel, but it will only be glued to the roof

Mark and cut corner angles for the roof

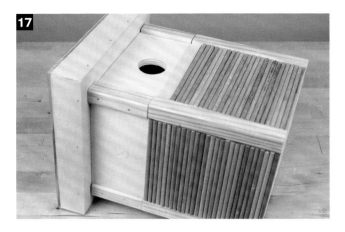

Glue and nail them in place

Spread glue over the surface of the roof wall...

...then start sticking pieces of dowel on the roof wall above the join board

Keep going until the top is reached. It doesn't matter that the hole is covered because it will be cut out later

Turn the roof around and repeat the process of sticking on pieces of dowel on the side

Continue all the way to the top, then finish the back and other side

Mark the position of the hole

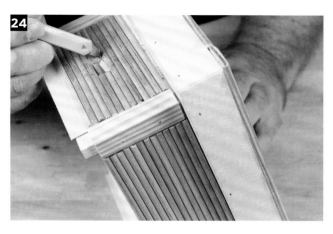

Use a sharp knife to cut out the dowel from in front of the hole

Sand the hole smooth with rolled-up sandpaper

Mark the position of the holes for the screws that will hold the roof to the box

Drill all four holes

The finished bamboo wall effect is completed and waiting for its finish

Doors, windows and other features

ALL THE FEATURES DESCRIBED IN THIS CHAPTER ARE DESIGNED TO MAKE YOUR BIRD HOUSE MORE APPEALING. THEY ARE NOT FUNCTIONAL AND DO NOT NEED NAILS. THE FEATURES ARE ADDED AFTER THE WALL TREATMENTS AND STUCK USING WATERPROOF GLUE OR HOT GLUE. YOU CAN MIX AND MATCH ANY WAY YOU LIKE AND PERFECT YOUR CUSTOM BIRD HOUSE WITH THESE FEATURES OR USE ONES OF YOUR OWN.

What you need

- Angle cutters
- Saws
- Waterproof wood glue
- Hot glue gun with glue
- Pencil
- Sharp knife
- 100 grit sandpaper (and wooden block)
- Tape measure
- Ruler
- Masking tape
- Combination square
- Hole saw of the diameter you require
- Drill
- Clamp
- Relevant wood and materials for each feature

An attention to detail is needed to make these small pieces

Doors

The front door is the entryway to a home – and although our bird house doors are purely decorative, they do look the part. The styles we have here should give you enough options to be creative with each of the bird house variations. The items here are made using the wood from the craft packs and cut to size with a knife or saw then trimmed to length using angle cutters.

Plank door

First cut a backboard at 3½in (90mm) high by 2in (50mm) wide. This is the base the door will be built on. Next cut a header frame at 2in (50mm) long from a ¼in (6mm) wide strip and glue it at the top of the backboard.

Some of the materials and tools needed to make the plank door

Mark the door backboard 2in (50mm) wide

Extend the line and cut to width

Mark 3½in (90mm) for the height of the door

Extend the line across the backboard and cut to length

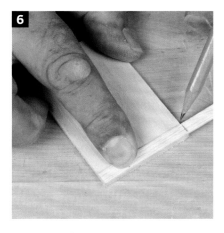

Mark the top part of the door frame to length

Cut to length using the angle cutters at 90°

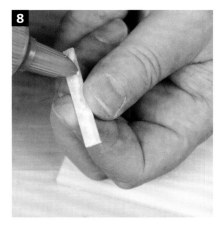

Glue the top door frame strip…

…and place it on the top on the backboard

Then, cut two upright frames from ¼in (6mm) wide strips and glue them in place on the edges of the backboard. Now, using some of the ⅜in (10mm) wide strips, cut them to the door length inside the frame and with a file or piece of sandpaper sand the corners off the front to create a chamfer (a 45° angle on the edge). Glue these boards to the backboard and fill the gap between the frame uprights.

You can finish there if you want as this is now a good-looking plank door with V-grooves, but you could add a porthole feature by cutting a hole in the door boards. When finished, paint or stain the door how you want and then add some blobs of glue on the back. Now stick it in place on the wall of the bird house where you want it.

Mark the height of the sides of the door frame

Cut the sides to length and stick them on either side of the backboard

Sand a chamfer on strips of ⅜in (10mm) wide strips

Mark the strips to length

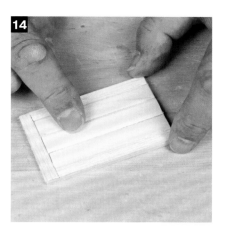

Cut and fit the strips between the frame

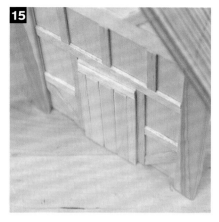

The door will be glued to the house after painting

Ledge door

This door is actually inside out as the ledges would typically be on the inside of the house, but using artistic licence we have put them on the outside for extra charm. The door is the same as the plank door but with ledges added. Cut two ⅜in (10mm) wide ledges at 1⅛in (30mm) long and glue them on the door, about ½in (12mm) away from the top and bottom of the door. When finished, paint or stain the door how you want it and then add some blobs of glue on the back. Now stick it in place on the wall of the bird house where you want it.

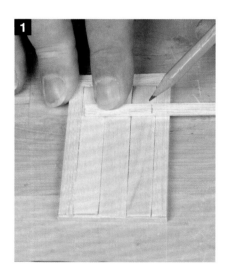

Mark and cut two 1⅛in (30mm) long ledges from ⅜in (10mm) wide strips

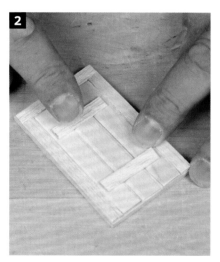

Glue them on the door about ½in (12mm) away from the top and bottom of the door

The plank door with ledges adds extra charm to the bird house

Panel door

A panel door is often paired with the style of building. To make a panel door, cut a backboard at 3½in (90mm) high by 2in (50mmm) wide. This is what we will build our door on. Make the frame first from ¼in (6mm) wide strips. Cut the header piece the full width of the backboard (2in/50mm), and glue it in place at the top of the backboard. Continue with the frame uprights; cut them to length and glue them in place.

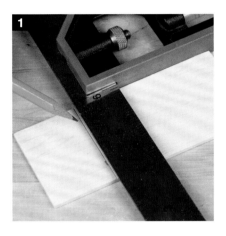

Mark and cut the 3½in (90mm) high by 2in (50mm) wide backboard

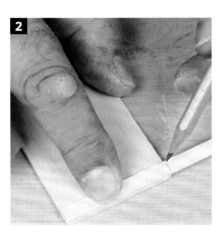

Mark the door frame head at the width of the backboard

Mark and cut the frame uprights and glue them all in place

Now make the door's stiles (the vertical parts of the outer frame) and rails (the horizontal parts of the outer frame). All the parts are made of ¼in (6mm) wide strips apart from the bottom rail, which is wider at ⅜in (10mm) wide. Cut the two upright pieces and glue them on the backboard next to the door frames. Now cut the top and middle rails from ¼in (6mm) strips and the bottom rail from a ⅜in (10mm) strip. Glue the top and bottom rail right at the top and bottom on the backboard but glue the middle rail just below the centre of the door and the panel door look is complete. Paint or stain the door how you want and then add some blobs of glue on the back. Now stick it in place on the wall of the bird house where you want it.

Mark the length of the door stile

Cut two stiles and glue them inside the door frame

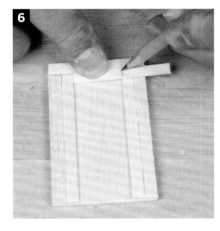

Mark the top rail

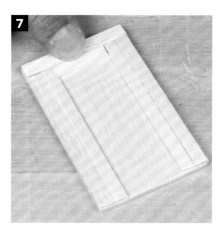

Cut the top rail and glue it in place at the top of the door

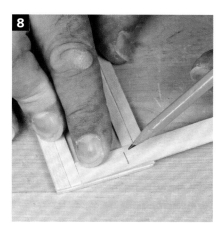

Mark the bottom rail from a wider strip

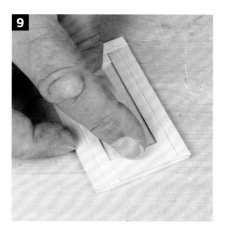

Cut and glue it in place

Now mark the middle mullion (the intermediate component on the wooden panel)

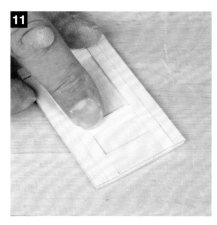

Cut and glue it in place towards the lower part of the door

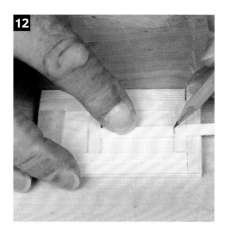

Mark the vertical mullion

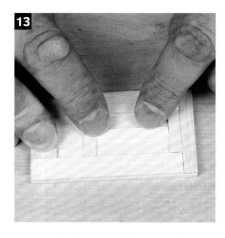

Cut and glue it in place in the centre of the door

The finished door now looks very realistic

The panel door is smart enough for a brick house

Windows

Cute windows will really enhance the look of the bird house. Although there are many different styles of window for you to choose from, I decided to make just two versions of a simple window with glass dividing bars to make either two- or four-pane versions.

Two- and four-pane windows

The start of the windows is to cut the backboard from a sheet of the wood from the craft pack. Make it 2 x 2in (50 x 50mm) square. This is a size that looks in scale on the side of the bird house. Mark and cut the two vertical stiles and glue and stick them to the sides of the backboard. Now, mark, cut, glue and stick the top and bottom rails at the top and bottom of the backboard in between the stiles. The two-pane window is now complete.

Cut the window backboard to size

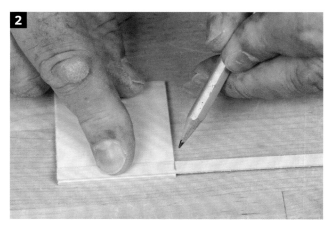

Mark the two window stiles...

...cut them to length...

...then glue them...

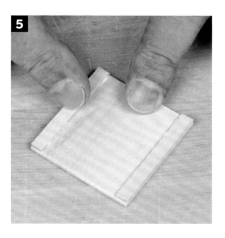

...and stick them to the sides of the backboard

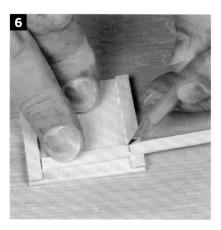

Now, mark and cut the two rails...

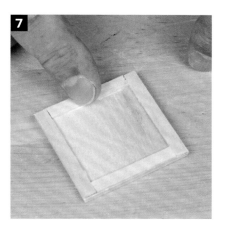

...then glue and stick them to the top and bottom of the backboard in between the stiles

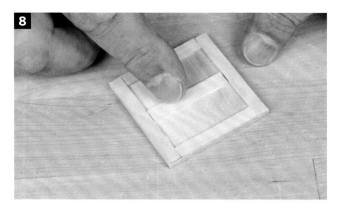

Mark and cut a central muntin, then glue it horizontally in the middle of the window. The two-pane window is now complete

To make the four-pane window, cut another horizontal rail the length of between the stiles and glue it in place halfway up the window. Now cut two short muntins (the vertical or horizontal components between glass panes) to fit vertically between the middle rail and the upper and lower rails, then glue them in place. The four-pane window is now complete.

Make all the windows you need and paint them before gluing them to your bird house.

For the four-pane window mark and cut two small muntins

Glue them in place vertically above and below the middle muntin; the four-pane window is now complete

Shutters

Storm protection is a must in some countries and window shutters are fitted to close over the windows for protection when a storm is brewing. They are simply hinged and latched in place over the windows when needed and folded back open again when the storm has passed. Two types of shutter are made here; one is a louvre style shutter suitable for a grand house, the other is a ledge shutter that is more suited to a rustic domicile.

Louvre shutters

Start by cutting a backboard to size. This is 2⅜in (60mm) high and 1in (25mm) wide. Each window will need two of them. Now cut two lengths of ¼in (6mm) wide strip for the vertical stiles and glue them in place on either side of the backboard.

Cut two strips for the top and bottom rails and glue and stick them in place at the top and bottom of the backboard. These louvres do not overlap like the ones on full-size houses, but are being made to emulate them.

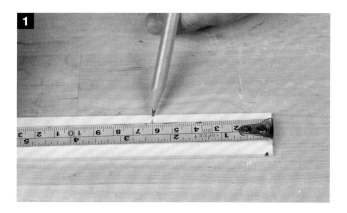

Mark the louvre backboard to size

Cut two of them per window

Mark the stile to the height of the backboard

Cut two of them to length

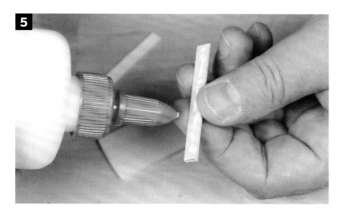

Glue along the back of the stile

Stick the two stiles to the backboard on either side

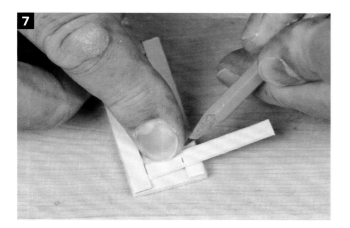

Mark the top and bottom rails to length

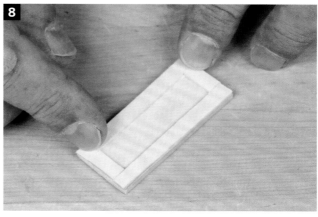

Glue them and place them at the top and bottom of the backboard

Take some ¼in (6mm) wide strip and sand a curve on one of its faces. When these are next to each other it will look like they overlap. Cut around nine pieces of this to fit between the vertical stiles and glue them in place on the backboard. The last piece may be too wide so it will need cutting down to fit. When this last piece is in place, the shutter is completed. Make all the shutters you need and paint them your preferred colour.

The louvres do not overlap like real ones, so we emulate the effect by sanding a curve on the top face of the ¼in (6mm) strip

Mark the louvre strips the distance between the stiles

Cut nine of them for each shutter

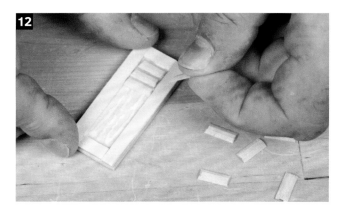

Glue and place them on the backboard

The last one may need cutting to width to fill the gap. Do this with the angle cutters

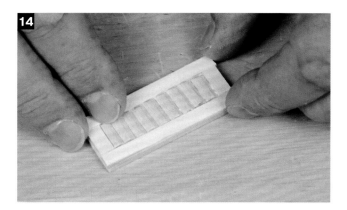

Stick the last piece in place

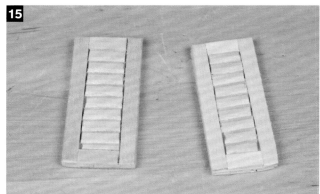

The two louvre shutters are ready to be painted and fitted

Ledge shutters

Ledge shutters are quite easy to make. First cut the backboard 2⅜in (60mm) high and 1in (25mm) wide and cut two shutters for each window. The vertical boards are made from ¼in (6mm) strips and have a chamfer sanded on their edges. A V-joint look is created when they are butted together. Cut four of these pieces for each shutter and they will be 2⅜in (60mm) long. Glue them to the backboard and they should fit across its width. If they are a bit narrow, just space them apart a little.

Mark the backboard to size

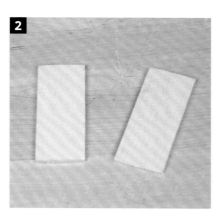

Cut two of them for each window

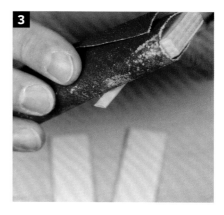

Sand chamfers on strips for the vertical boards so a V-groove is created when they butt together

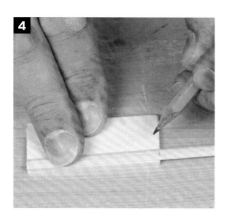

Mark the vertical boards to length

Cut them using the angle cutters

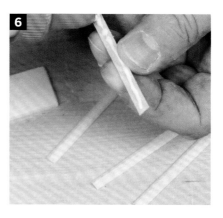

Make four vertical boards for each shutter and run a line of glue on them

Glue them to the backboard

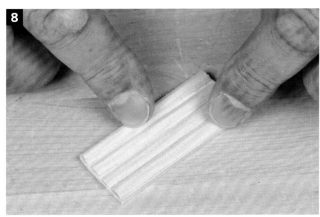

The four pieces should be the right width for the backboard

Cut two ledges from a ¼in (6mm) strip at ¾in (19mm) long, then chamfer their front edges and ends. Glue the ledges and place them ⅜in (10mm) from each end. The shutter is now complete. Make as many shutters as you need and paint them.

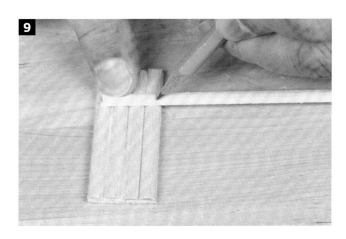

Mark the length of the ledge

Cut two ledges, sand their ends with a chamfer and glue them on the shutters at ⅜in (10mm) from each end

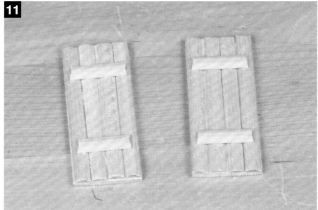

A pair of shutters will look great on rustic houses

Portico

A portico is an elegant feature designed to make an entranceway look more grandiose. It is built round the front door and consists of a roof with walls or columns flanking it. It is not only decorative, but will also provide shelter from the weather when entering the front door.

Making the portico

The portico is built on a backboard. The backboard I used is one of the thinner sheets of wood I found in the craft pack. Cut the backboard 3⅛in (80mm) wide and initially at 5in (137mm) tall for now; its final height will be determined later. At the centre of the board, mark a vertical line above where the door will be placed. Then, at 3¼in (85mm) high on the backboard edges mark a 45° line to the centre mark on both sides. Cut the backboard on these lines to give the 90° pitch for the portico roof.

You need a sheet of wood for the backboard and roof, and a piece of ½ x ¼in (12 x 6mm) strip for the side columns to make the portico

Mark the backboard at 3⅛in (80mm) wide. This will fit comfortably around the door

Mark the centre of the backboard above the door

At 3¼in (85mm) high on the edges, mark a 45° line to the centre mark using the square

Repeat this on the other side to create a 90° angle

Cut the backboard on the line to create the pitch for the portico roof

Cut the portico's side columns at 3¼in (85mm) long and glue them edgewise on the side of the backboard. Now cut the roof pieces at 1in (25mm) wide and 2⅝in (65mm) long and glue them to the backboard and on top of the columns. Apply plenty of glue and hold the pieces in place with masking tape until the glue dries. When the glue is dry, run a bead of glue around the inside of the roof and columns again and this will give it strength. The portico can be painted a colour to suit your bird house scheme. The door is glued in the portico to finish the job.

Mark and cut the side columns at 3¼in (85mm) long

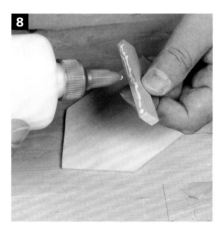

Run a line of glue along the edge of the column…

…then stick it on the side of the backboard

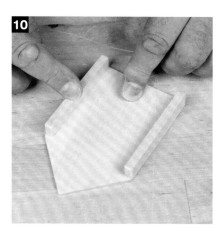

Repeat this for the other column

Mark and cut two 1in (25mm) wide strips at 2⅝in (65mm) long for the portico roof

Glue the ends of the roof where they will meet

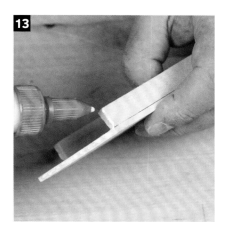

Glue the tops of the columns and along the edges of the backboard's pitch

Place the roof pieces together at 90° and stick on a piece of masking tape to hold the joint

Place the roof on the backboard and columns. Hold it for a while for the glue to start drying

Run a line of glue all around the inside edges of where the roof meets the other pieces to give more strength

This is how the grandiose portico looks in position. It is ready for painting

Porthole

A porthole is normally associated with boats and ships, and a round window is ideal for this type of structure. A porthole window or surround on a house can give it a maritime look but is also a nice way to finish a window in a gable end where a rectangular window would not really work.

The porthole is a surround that gives a finishing touch to the bird house entrance hole, but could also be used as a resizer to attract a different size of bird. If you have previously built a bird house with a large hole to attract bigger birds and you now want to attract smaller ones, there is no need to build a whole new house. You can simply make a porthole surround with a smaller hole.

Making the porthole

To make the porthole, I have used a piece of wood from the craft pack. I wanted the outside diameter to be 2in (50mm), so I found a container lid that was the correct size and used it to draw the circle on the board. I then marked the centre of the circle, which will be the centre point for the 1⅛in (30mm) hole saw. Drill the hole before cutting the outside circle so there is plenty of wood to hold onto while drilling. It can help to clamp the board to the bench before doing this.

Use a block of wood behind the board to protect the bench and drill halfway through the board.

Use a 2in (50mm) diameter container lid (or similar) to draw the external size on the board

Draw round the container lid

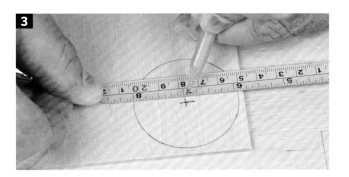

Mark the centre of the drawn circle

Using the 1⅛in (30mm) hole saw, carefully cut the hole in the board, but only halfway through

Turn the board over and drill through the board. This turning process helps reduce tearout and creates a cleaner hole. Next, clamp the wood to the bench and cut out the outer circle. I used a coping saw but you could use a powered scrollsaw, if you have one. The last thing to do is clean up the porthole by sanding off the rough edges. A piece of rolled-up sandpaper takes care of the inside hole.

Sandpaper wrapped around a block will enable you to sand the outside of the circle to make it even after sawing. Finally, the edges should be smoothed off.

The finished porthole can now be painted and fitted around the entrance hole.

Turn the board over and finish drilling the hole. Tearout is reduced by cutting from both sides

Hold the board and cut the outer diameter. A coping saw may be useful here

The porthole is cut out but has rough edges

Sand around the inside of the hole to smooth off the rough edges

Sand around the outside of the porthole to even up the circle and smooth the edges

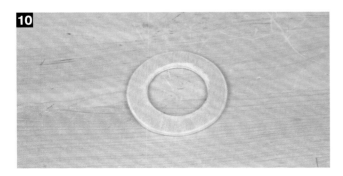

The finished porthole

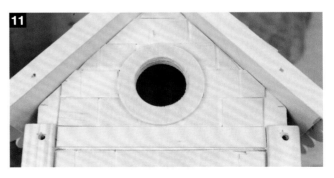

The porthole looks great in the gable end of a bird house. It is now ready for painting

Paint and finish

IT IS GOOD PRACTICE TO APPLY A THICK WHITE WATER-BASED BASE COAT TO THE INSIDE AND OUTSIDE OF YOUR BIRD HOUSE TO SEAL THE WOOD. THIS HELPS TO MAKE IT WATERTIGHT BEFORE YOU APPLY A FINISH. I USE WATER-BASED PRODUCTS SO THERE ARE NO FUMES THAT WOULD HARM THE BIRDS, AND THEY ARE EASY TO CLEAN UP AFTERWARDS.

What you need

- Selection of paintbrushes
- Selection of paint sponges
- Selection of paint colours (water-based as a preference)
- Masking tape
- Paint stands (painter's pyramids)

Setting up

This first coat of paint gives a good base for any colour you want to finish your bird house with. Painting is your opportunity to be creative and make your bird house the most attractive feature of your garden. You may want to paint your bird house in colours that are traditional for the style of your house – or you may have other ideas. There are no rules here, so do be adventurous.

If you prefer to keep your bird house unpainted use an outdoor deck water-based finish, possibly with a stain in it, and coat the house inside and out. A couple of coats will be enough. I used the deck finish for the parts I wanted left in a natural wood finish. I also got a mix of paint colours from the craft store and these proved useful for mixing my own colours for the individual features and details.

Standard primer and outdoor deck finishes are suitable for the base coat. Painter's pyramids are used to keep parts off the ground while painting

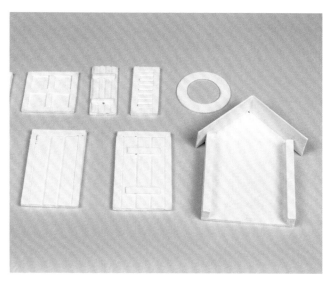

Paint the doors, windows and other features white

An eye for detail helps while painting

A selection of paints, brushes and sponges is useful

Horizontal siding

A horizontal siding is usually painted in pastel or bright colours with a contrasting white trim and individual features. The base coat is white so you just need to fill in with the colour of your choice, taking care to cut a clean edge on the trim. You might want to use masking tape for this, but if you have a sharp paintbrush and a steady hand there is no need for that. The door is enhanced with bright red paint. The roof used on this bird house is the slant roof with the grass covering. The siding is painted the same colour as the base and the trim boards and porthole are left white.

The bird house in wood

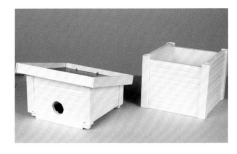

The outside of the bird house in base coat

The inside of the bird house in base coat

Photocopy this illustration and colour it in so you can experiment with colour

The finished painted front of the bird house

The finished painted back of the bird house

Vertical metal siding

A vertical metal siding is often used on industrial or agricultural buildings. It will usually be a rather dull grey, but I particularly like the bright red paint often seen on barns in rural America. The corner mouldings are white to give a nice contrast and make them stand out. The roof chosen for this house is the curved one with the shingle covering. The siding is matched to the box, with the porthole and trim left white. The shingles could have been left natural and the deck finish applied to it, but I decided to paint them a darker brown as it was better suited to the barn effect.

The bird house in wood

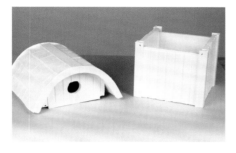

The outside of the bird house in base coat

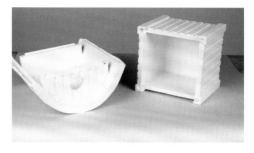

The inside of the bird house in base coat

Photocopy this illustration and colour it in so you can experiment with colour

The finished painted front of the bird house

The finished painted back of the bird house

Tudor-style beams

The traditional style of a Tudor home is to have black beams with white walls. Paint the bird house white, both inside and out, then paint the beams. A sharp brush with a steady hand is needed to cut the edges of the beams to the white of the background. All individual features such as windows and doors are painted a dark brown to emulate wood. The roof chosen for this bird house is the thatched pitch roof. The roof was painted white inside and out, apart from the black beams, but the deck finish was applied to the thatch covering to give it a natural look.

The bird house in wood

The outside of the bird house in base coat

The inside of the bird house in base coat

Photocopy this illustration and colour it in so you can experiment with colour

The finished painted front of the bird house

The finished painted back of the bird house

Log cabin

In order to retain its natural wood appearance, the log cabin is enhanced using several coats of deck finish. Apply a liberal coat of deck finish all over the log cabin's surface treatment. When dry, apply another coat to ensure full coverage and maximize how waterproof the house will be. The individual features such as windows and doors were painted a dark green to complete the wilderness log cabin look. The pitch tin roof was chosen for this bird house and was painted a dark grey to emulate a tin finish. Tin roofs are also painted other colours, so you can be adventurous and try other options.

The bird house in wood

The outside of the bird house in base coat and deck finish

The inside of the bird house in base coat and deck finish

Photocopy this illustration and colour it in so you can experiment with colour

The finished painted front of the bird house

The finished painted back of the bird house

Brick walls

Brick houses have a sealing coat of white paint, both inside and out. After the base coat has been applied, select the colour of brick you would like. The best way to achieve a brick appearance is by using a flat sponge pad and blotting the paint onto the walls. You could leave the corner mouldings white to contrast with the brick. I chose a yellow for the individual features and a darker brown for the portico roof. The pitch tile roof has its tiles painted a darker colour so they are different from the brick. The porthole and roof trim are the same yellow as the individual features of the box.

The bird house in wood

The outside of the bird house in base coat

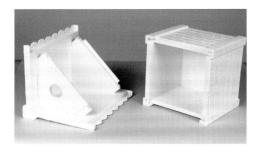

The inside of the bird house in base coat

Photocopy this illustration and colour it in so you can experiment with colour

The finished painted front of the bird house

The finished painted back of the bird house

Bamboo walls

The dowel used to create the bamboo look is coated in the deck finish, both inside and out. The individual features are painted a pale green as this house lends itself to a calming feel. This bird house would work well in an oriental garden and wind chimes might help to give a peaceful ambience. The flat solar roof has the same deck finish for the bamboo and the pale green is used on the roof surround. The solar panel is inconspicuous and sits out of the way in its recess.

Bird house in wood

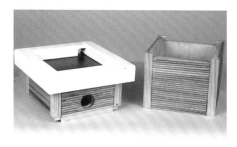

The outside of the bird house in base coat and deck finish

The inside of the bird house in base coat and deck finish

Photocopy this illustration and colour it in so you can experiment with colour

The finished painted front of the bird house

The finished painted back of the bird house

Base treatment

CUSTOM-MADE BIRD HOUSES MAKE FINE HOMES FOR ANY BIRD FAMILY TO MOVE INTO. HOWEVER, YOU MIGHT WANT TO TAKE THINGS A STEP FURTHER AND MAKE THEM EVEN MORE DECORATIVE BY ADDING A BASE THAT WILL ACT AS A SMALL GARDEN OR YARD. SOME MINIATURE DECORATIVE ITEMS CAN ALSO BE ADDED AND THESE ARE READILY AVAILABLE FROM CRAFT STORES OR ONLINE.

What you need

- 1 x ⅜in (10mm) thick plywood x 8¼in (210mm) deep x 9in (230mm) wide
- Waterproof glue
- Angle cutters
- Drill and drill bit to match screw diameter
- 4 x wood screws ¾in (19mm) long
- Pre-made fence pieces
- Selection of miniature items from craft store

Making the base

The first thing to do is to cut a baseboard for everything to be added to. When cut to size, this is a little bigger than the footprint of the house. I made this one 8¼in (210mm) deep x 9in (230mm) wide, cut from ½in (12mm) thick plywood. Then drill four holes in it so it can be screwed to the bottom of the bird house, make sure the screws you use do not protrude into the bird house as the occupants won't like that.

A selection of items chosen to enhance the look of the bird house

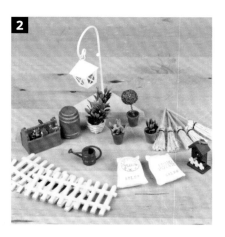

The selected items unpacked

Mark and cut a piece of ⅜in (10mm) thick plywood slightly larger than the bird house at 8¼in (210mm) deep x 9in (230mm) wide

Cut it to size then drill four holes to screw the base to the underside of the bird house

In the decorative packs I got from the craft store there were some picket fence pieces about 3in (75mm) long. There is nothing more traditional in the USA than a white picket fence. I was going to make a fence from strips of wood glued together, but these pieces save a lot of time in making something that will only be seen from a distance.

If you want to create a gate in front of the door, cut a piece of the fence flush with the outside of two of the uprights and a little wider than the door. Now cut the pieces to go either side of it, first trimming off the ends of the horizontal rail so the vertical pieces butt up to each side of the gate. Trim them to the width of the baseboard (when all placed together) and glue them to the edge of the base. Continue cutting and gluing the fence all around the baseboard. You may need to cut small pieces to make it all fit. I placed small blocks of wood in front of the fence pieces to hold them in place while the glue dried. When the glue is dry, the whole base can be painted white.

Mark the pieces first before cutting to create a gate in the fence in front of the door

Cut the pieces with the angle cutters

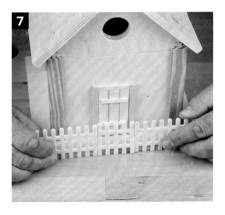

Place the pieces alongside each other to make sure they fit

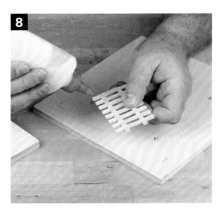

Glue the bottom part of the fence

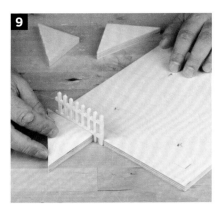

Position the fence on the edge of the base and place a block of wood in front to hold it in place while the glue dries

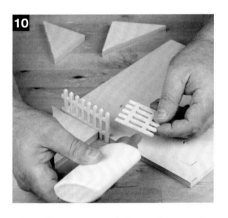

Glue the gate and the other end fence piece

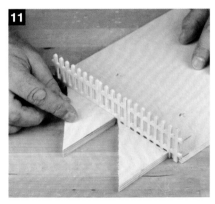

Place them next to the first piece on the base edge and hold in place with another block of wood

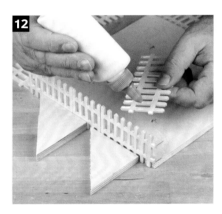

Glue the ends of the fence and the rails where the next piece turns the corner

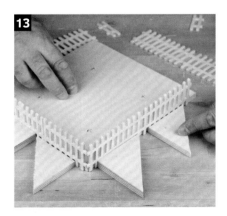

Keep gluing and adding more fence pieces

Cut small pieces, if needed, to make up the distance along the base edge

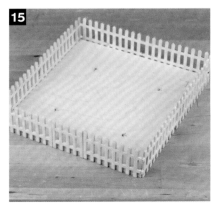

Continue all around the base until it is completely fenced in

16

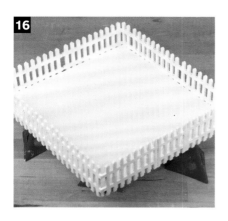

Paint the base and the picket fence white

When the paint is dry, the base can be screwed onto the bottom of the bird house. Decorating it is immense fun with the miniature items that you can choose to match the style of your house. See a selection of my choices, but you can let your imagination run wild to create a truly unique bird house.

17

Place a bird house on the base and screw in place, making sure that the screws don't protrude into the bird house. It is now ready to decorate

18

Sacks of flour and the rain barrel enhance the barn look

19

A rain barrel, toolbox and lamp complete the log cabin

20

The brick house has plants and its own mini bird house

21

The grass roof house has plants, a watering can and broom

22

A water barrel and sacks of grain decorate the Tudor-style house

23

The bamboo house is decorated with plants and an outdoor lamp

Mounting your bird house

ONCE YOU HAVE CREATED YOUR BIRD HOUSE YOU WILL WANT TO MOUNT IT SECURELY OUTSIDE. I HAVE CHOSEN METHODS AND MOUNTING OPTIONS THAT ARE SAFE TO USE AND EASY AND QUICK TO MAKE. THEY ARE ALSO VERSATILE WHEN FINDING A POSITION FOR YOUR BIRD HOUSE IN THE GARDEN. OF COURSE, IF YOU DON'T WANT BIRDS MOVING IN, BLANK OFF THE HOLE IN THE ROOF AND USE THE HOUSE FOR DECORATION ONLY.

What you need

The items you need will depend on your mounting option

- Galvanized metal conduit pipe, tapered thread ends (various lengths to suit mounting method)
- Galvanized metal conduit 90° elbow, two female threads
- Galvanized metal conduit 90° elbow, one male and one female thread
- Galvanized metal conduit connector, two female threads
- Galvanized metal conduit mounting plate
- Wood screws to mount plate (length to suit)
- Washers
- Predator baffle cone
- Grease, for making the pole slippery
- Lengths of chain
- Chain connectors
- 4 x eye hooks
- Pipe wrench
- Hammer/mallet
- Screwdriver
- Spirit level
- Tree, fence or garden space

Mounting methods

I decided to use galvanized steel pipe with a tapered thread on its ends as one method of mounting bird houses. Steel pipe is easily available from DIY or plumbing suppliers and the system is available in many different diameters. There are also plenty of options for joining pipes together with elbows and connectors and items called floor flanges that are ideal as mounting plates. The tapered threads ensure a tight fit can be achieved however the house is rotated, so it is easy to position the entrance of the house in any particular direction and the thread will be tight enough to hold it there. Being made of galvanized steel also ensures the pipe is extremely rust resistant. I chose the 1in (25mm) diameter pipe to use as it is inexpensive and sturdy enough for our purposes.

Before you start mounting the bird house, it is a good idea to screw the mounting plate to the bottom, then take it off. The holes are then ready for screwing it on again when mounting.

A collection of parts for various mounting options

Start by screwing the mounting plate to the bottom of the bird house, ready for mounting properly later

Tree mount

Mounting the bird house on the trunk of a tree is a very attractive option and is great for viewing and taking photographs.

Find a fairly vertical piece of tree trunk, facing more or less the direction you want your bird house to be. Screw the mounting plate onto the tree. If it isn't quite vertical you can use washers as spacers behind the mounting plate between it and the tree. Thread a short length of pipe into the mounting plate and tighten with a pipe wrench.

Select the elbow that has a protruding thread on one end and screw the other end on the horizontal pipe. Use the pipe wrench to ensure the external thread of the elbow is vertical. Thread the bird house mounting plate onto the elbow and lastly, screw the mounting plate to the base of the bird house. Use the screw holes prepared earlier and rotate the bird house so it is tight and pointing in the correct direction. Sit back, relax and enjoy watching your new wildlife friends.

Screw the elbow into the mounting plate under the bird house. A short pipe from that will attach to the mounting plate that will screw into the tree trunk

Screw the mounting plate to a relatively vertical part of the tree trunk. Washers can be used as spacers to level things up

Using a pipe wrench, screw a short length of pipe into the mounting plate

Tighten a 90° elbow joint with an external thread onto the horizontal pipe. Make sure the external thread end is vertical

Thread the mounting plate onto the elbow and screw the bird house onto the mounting plate, using the holes prepared earlier

The bird house looks delightful on this mount. It is in a great position for photo opportunities

Fence mount

A fence is another option for mounting a bird house. Although the height of the fence might be lower than you might like for your bird house, you can adjust the height of the bird house by using longer pipes.

Screw the mounting plate to the fence as high up as possible. Thread a longish pipe horizontally into the mounting plate and tighten it with the pipe wrench. Screw a coupling elbow onto the end of the pipe and tighten it so that its open end is vertical; the wrench will be useful for this too.

Now thread a piece of pipe into the elbow. This piece can be any length to position your bird house where you want it to be. Lastly, screw the mounting plate onto the vertical pipe and then to the underside of the bird house.

This is a good place to add a decorative base as the lower level means the base can be seen to its best advantage. This mounting method can be used on house walls too, but if your house is brick you will need to use a masonry drill and plugs for the screw in the mounting plate.

Screw a short pipe into the mounting plate and screw the elbow onto that. A longer pipe will then go between the elbow and the fence mounting plate

Screw the mounting plate onto the fence

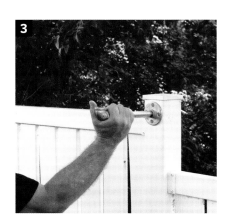

Thread a longer piece of pipe and the 90° elbow onto the mounting plate. Make sure the end of the elbow is vertical

Tighten a longer length of pipe and the mounting plate into the coupling elbow

Screw the mount to the bird house using the holes you prepared earlier

Pole mount

This is probably the best and safest way to mount your bird house. A pole can be positioned almost anywhere and then faced in any direction by simply rotating it. Using a single pole will deter predators as climbing the pole is the only way to get to the house. As a further deterrent, grease the pole or add a baffle cone that predators can't climb round.

Hammer a long pole into the ground. Its length will depend on the type of ground you have; my garden has dense soil so a 24in (600mm) long pole holds firmly. Use a spirit level to ensure that the pole is

perfectly upright. I used a rubber mallet but it is a good idea to thread the pipe connector on the end so it takes the pounding instead of the pipe.

Drive the pipe into the ground as far as the connector. Thread the pole into the connector and tighten using the pipe wrench. I used a 72in (1380mm) long pipe, but will probably add a longer piece to get the bird house a little higher. This is easily done using another connector and a short piece of pipe. Thread the mounting plate on top of the vertical pipe and the top of the bird house.

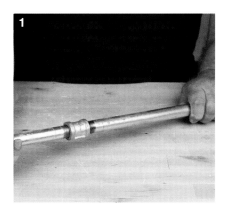

A connector makes it easy to join the long pipe to the pipe that has been driven into the ground

The long pipe screws into the mounting plate on the underside of the bird house

Take a length of pipe and drive it into the ground. Using a spirit level will make sure it is perfectly upright. The connector on the end protects the thread while being hammered

Drive the pipe in the ground until it is nice and firm

Thread the long pipe into the connector

Thread the mounting plate to the bottom of the bird house using the previously prepared holes

Hanging chain mount

The final mounting method is to use chain. A hanging bird house is an attractive way to mount it. Find a branch on your tree that is the correct height for it to go. Drill holes in either end of the roof of the bird house and then screw an eye hook into both the holes. Make sure the eyes are vertical for the chain to sit properly.

Cut two short pieces of chain (mine were 6in/ 150mm long) and slip an 'S'-shaped connector into each end of the chain and crimp it closed with a pair of pliers. Hook the connectors onto the eye hooks in the roof and crimp them closed there

too. Screw another eye hook into the underside of the branch you chose earlier, then slip the two connectors on the ends of the chain into the eye hook. There is no need to crimp them as gravity will hold them in place and you will also be able to take the bird house down when needed. You can get the bird house to face the direction you want it to by simply rotating the eye hook in the tree trunk.

This popular way to mount your bird house will sway in the wind so its occupants will be gently rocked to sleep.

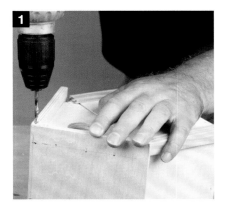

Drill holes in the ends of the roof for the eye hooks

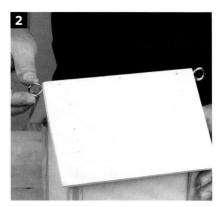

Screw in an eye hook at each end of the roof

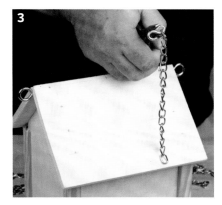

Crimp a piece of chain onto a connector

Crimp the connector onto the eye hook

Repeat on the other end and join them in the middle so they can be attached to another eye hook (which will be screwed into the underside of a tree branch)

Find a suitable branch and screw in an eye hook on its underside. Hang the bird house by its chain from the eye hook in the branch

Tree-mounted log cabin bird house with pitch tin roof

Bird house with grass roof and picket fence

Tree-mounted brick bird house with tile roof

Tree-mounted bamboo bird house with solar roof

Fence-mounted Tudor-style bird house

Pole-mounted bird house with bamboo walls

Tree-mounted bird house with horizontal siding

Log cabin bird house with hanging chain mount

Fence-mounted barn-style bird house

Tree-mounted bird house with thatched pitch roof and Tudor-style beams

About the author

Woodworker and journalist Alan Goodsell has written extensively on woodworking and tools for a range of magazines including the highly acclaimed *Woodturning*, *The Router*, *Furniture & Cabinetmaking* (GMC Publications) and *American Router* (Lightning Publications). A significant move took Alan to the USA, where he ran the Marketing Department for a top router bit and cutting tool manufacturer. Still living in Florida, Alan has moved back into publishing and is now producing a range of woodworking-related publications.

Acknowledgements

Special thanks to my fiancée, Betty Acero.

Picture credits

All pictures by the author except for the following images from Shutterstock:
Page 1: Bachkova Natalia; page 6 (top): Bachkova Natalia, (bottom): Sichon; page 10: AlekseyKarpenko; page 11: Bonnie Taylor Barry; page 12: Boyce's Images (ash-throated flycatcher), Steve Byland (downy woodpecker), Mircea Costina (tufted titmouse), Hayley Crews (Nuttall's woodpecker), FotoRequest (hairy woodpecker), Tom Reichner (great crested flycatcher), Jon Stager (chickadee); page 13: Bruce MacQueen (white-breasted nuthatch), Paul Reeves Photography (red-breasted nuthatch), Ed Schneider (prothonotary warbler and yellow-bellied sapsucker), Takahashi Photography (western bluebird), vagabond54 (pygmy nuthatch), Tim Zurowski (mountain bluebird); page 14: Brian E Kushner (house wren), Glenn Price (Carolina wren), raulbaenacasado (Bewick's wren), David Spates (violet-green swallow), Gregg Williams (tree swallow); page 15: ArCaLu (great tit), Sharon Day (house sparrow), Garrett Gibson (starling), Johannes Dag Mayer (tree sparrow), rbrechko (blue tit), Monika Surzin (nuthatch), Klaas Vledder (pied flycatcher); page 19 (top right): Steve Byland, (bottom): Joerg Lue; page 20: Nick Vorobey; page 28: Victor Tyakht; page 46: Steve Byland; page 80: Victor Tyakht; page 118: AlekseyKarpenko; page 136: Bachkova Natalia; page 144: AlekseyKarpenko; page 148: FloridaStock.

Index

First published 2019 by
Guild of Master Craftsman Publications Ltd
Castle Place, 166 High Street, Lewes,
East Sussex, BN7 1XU, UK

ISBN 978 1 78494 519 0

A catalogue record for this book is available from the
British Library.

Publisher: Jonathan Bailey
Production: Jim Bulley and Jo Pallett
Senior Project Editor: Sara Harper
Editor: Sarah Doughty
Managing Art Editor: Gilda Pacitti
Art Editor: Manisha Patel
Photographer: Alan Goodsell
Illustrators: Randall Maxey; Alex Bailey (pages 138–43)
Craft Assistant: Maria Nobregas

Colour origination by GMC Reprographics
Printed and bound in China

To order a book, or to request a catalogue, contact:

GMC Publications Ltd, Castle Place, 166 High Street,
Lewes, East Sussex, BN7 1XU, UK
Tel: +44 (0)1273 488005

www.gmcbooks.com